ONE HEROIC HOUR
at KING'S MOUNTAIN

PAT ALDERMAN

Second Edition
(INDEX ADDED)

Battle of King's Mountain
October 7, 1780

The battle that changed the course of American History.

The Overmountain Press
JOHNSON CITY, TENNESSEE

FROM ORIGINAL PUBLICATION

Bibliography: Lyman C. Draper, *King's Mountain and its Heroes;* J.G.M. Ramsey, *Annals of Tennessee;* John P. Brown, *Old Frontiers;* Daughters of the American Revolution, Various Publications; John Haywood, *Civil and Political History of Tennessee;* North Carolina Records, *Publications of the Historical Commission;* Lewis P. Summers, *History of Southwest Virginia;* Tennessee Historical Society, Various Publications; Samuel Cole Williams, *Tennessee During Revolutionary War;* Katherine Keogh White, *The King's Mountain Men;* Sara Sullivan Ervin, *South Carolinians in the Revolution;* Lucian Lamar Knight, *Georgia's Roster of the Revolution;* D.A.R., *Roster of Soldiers from North Carolina in the Revolution.*

Acknowledgments: Edyth Price; William D. Bowman; Joe Olivares; Orby Walker; Malcom Fowler; Ayers collection, Newberry Library; Charles Pugh; King's Mountain National Military Park; Ben Moomaw; James Anderson; Fred Woods; Bernie Andrews; J.P. Brown's *Old Frontiers*; Williams' *Dawn of Tennessee Valley*; and special thanks to Charles Crockett for script reading and helpful advice.

Cover Art by Timothy N. Tate

THE OVERMOUNTAIN MEN

Pat Alderman   Verna Alderman

We come ov-er the high moun-tain look-ing for the prom-ised land_

Dim trails ev-er lead-ing west-ward Nar-row steep and treach-er-ous

Sun and moon beat down up-on us Dan-ger lurks on ev-ry hand_ Brave men

Nev-er look-ing back-ward as we fol-low un-known trails Ov-er the hills

Down thru the vales fol-low-ing the riv-ers fear-less on our way peo-ple seek-ing

free-dom lands to build a home West-ward and on-ward to lands un-known

Battle of King's Mountain
October 7, 1780

Contents

Like specters from out of nowhere came an army of patriots and pioneers. It was not an army by military standards. It had no uniforms; its guns, though not obsolete, were a hodge-podge variety of flintlock and musket, each weapon exhibiting extreme degrees of durability and class but each weapon and owner were an independent entity. Esprit de corps was a strange expression to these people, but yet the competence and pride that each man felt toward his own ability and the ability of his comrade in arms, without the fatal complacency, was an awesome factor for the British.

But this little army that wasn't an army destroyed a superior force in material and number, and then, like the miracle army it was, faded into the mountain mists.

The apparition the British saw at King's Mountain October 7, 1780 was no apparition at all, but an integrated force of flesh and muscle and sinew, wedded to one common purpose and directed by the destiny of a growing nation.

The Revolutionary War from beginning to end was very unmilitary; and by contemporary standards its battles were mere skirmishes.

But never was a call to arms more eloquent, no appeal so fraught with logic, no cause more drastic, no victory more demanding, no challenge more inspiring, than the Tory threat to the peace and independency of America.

The results have reverberated down through the years and each succeeding generation of descendants of those mighty men takes increasing pride in the contribution their glorious ancestors played in uniting this nation.

Moral issues were at stake — and independence. A vision from the mountain top had given them an insight of greatness; and although they were a combination of heterogeneous cultures seeking a free and independent democracy, they fought as great men and left a great imprint on history.

The battlefield was their hearthstone. Clear of mind, pure of thought, determined and resolved, these sturdy people met the enemy and he was theirs. And by their conduct on that memorable day, the foundation of a great government was laid.

The patriotic half of young America who fought and supported the War was endowed with a broad outlook. The other half was opposed to the fight for freedom and the attendant responsibilities of self-rule that it would impose.

They feared reprisals and recriminations by the British; they resented the privations and loss of income from a long and tedious fight. They were non-committal to the patriots and attempted an attitude of neutrality where the British were concerned. A third of the population of the new America were out-and-out Tories. Congress did not have the ability or authority to wage this war. It was in reality a fight between thirteen individual Colonial States against the trained professionals of England. The Patriots had to fight a three-front war: one against their Tory neighbors; a second with the Indians, allies of the British, who threatened their rear; and, of course, the Loyalist regiments, commanded and supplied by the Royal Empire.

The New England and the Southern phases of the Revolutionary War were entirely different in cause and intent. All thirteen States had differing interests. Their unity was geographical and not political. Their one common bond was liberty and freedom from English oppression.

Thus the year 1780 was almost a disastrous and overwhelming one for Congress and the Americans. The war in the New England States was at a stalemate. The British had moved into the South and were fast overrunning Georgia and the Carolinas. General Cornwallis and his growing army seemed invincible. No organized resistance seemed possible. Then, Saturday afternoon, October 7, 1780, about three o'clock, came a thunderbolt that changed the course of history.

The King's Mountain victory looms with even greater significance when viewed through international intrigue of 1778-1783. France and Spain were secretly helping America, not because of brotherly love or friendship, but to hurt England. Benjamin Franklin and Silas Deane were earnestly seeking open allies to aid their struggling country. The victory at Saratoga, and Franklin's persuasive arguments, overrode the one hundred and fifty years of enmity the French had for the colonists. French leaders saw a selfish opportunity to embarrass England on another front, and, at the same time, protect French possessions in North America. They agreed to furnish troops, ships and money. But, had the French leaders realized their support of republicanism would hasten the fall of their own monarchy, they would have perhaps joined forces with England and helped destroy America.

Spain would not espouse the American cause, Florida Blanca, the Spanish Minister, hated England and all Americans. One of Spain's conditions in their alliance with France, was the agreement that the Mississippi Valley would be Spain's. All during the dismal year of 1780, Blanca was pressuring Congress, through the French Representative, for a cession of at least part of the Mississippi Valley.

The successful campaign of the British in the south caused the government of Lord North to project the forming of the Carolinas, Georgia, and the Bahamas into a separate Colonial Territory. The rule of international law was: "Hold by Force." Each of the powers wanted to control as much territory as possible.

During all this back stage maneuvering, Franklin kept selling the advantages to be obtained by helping America. His personal magnetism won the support needed and so some prominent men — Lafayette and de Kalb, French officers; Pulaski and Kosciuszko from Poland; and German von Steuben — became great names in American history. They, like Franklin and Deane, were aware of the growing strength and vitality of the young republic. But few of the world leaders realized that the loose federation of states would one day grow into a strong union that would influence the policies of the world.

**Marquis
De Lafayette**

**Barron
de Kalb**

**Count
Pulaski**

**Thaddeus
Kosciusko**

**Baron
von Steuben**

Now quoting from Bancroft, "we come to the series of events which closed the American contest and restored peace to the world...France was straining every nerve to cope with her rival Britain in the four quarters of the globe; Spain was exhausting her resources for the conquest of Gibralter; but the incidents which overthrew the Ministry of Lord North and reconciled Great Britain to America, had their springs in South Carolina."

The King's Mountain battle was not the most strategic victory of the Revolutionary War, but it was the most decisive. One year and twelve days afterwards, General Cornwallis surrendered in Yorktown, Virginia. The men of this Ghost Legion constituted the last effective resistance to the British onslaught. These Overmountain frontiersmen were not trained soldiers, and military discipline was practically unknown. They belonged to small local companies of pioneer settlers, organized under their own leader, to protect the frontiers from Indian raids. Their one common interest was family and home. Every man and officer fought for himself, and the best officers were those who fought best; they were leaders rather than commanders. When fighting was in progress the officer was expected to be up front. Failure to do this would indicate cowardice, and he would be removed from command by acclamation rather than court-martial. When a leader thought a campaign was needed for the common good, he would send riders to summon the men to prearranged muster ground. They would come mounted and equipped at their own expense, expecting no government pay. Living in their primitive independence, behind their tall mountain barrier, they had scant knowledge of the war raging along the eastern seaboard.

These frontiersmen were sons of frontiersmen, accustomed to the rugged life of the new country. They were courageous souls, daring and eager as they ventured along the unfamiliar trails leading westward. The wide expanse of mountains, hills and valleys, covered with virgin forests and teeming with wild game, challenged their pioneer spirits. This unhampered wilderness freedom, far removed from royal rulers and their taxes, was to their liking. These bold, resolute men were self-reliant. They were independent, individualistic, and not always inclined to respect or observe the niceties of the soft life. Living on the outskirts of civilization, their law was to have and to hold. They depended on the forest and streams for their sustenance. They would pitch a fight, scalp an Indian or wrestle ("rassel") a bear at the drop of a hat.

This mountaineer force did not dress in the general military fashion of the day. The long fringed hunting shirt was worn by most of the pioneer army, and was usually made of dressed deer skin, very Indian in looks and use. It was made with an opening in front with plenty of overlap. A leather or wampum type belt fastened around the waist would hold it together, and at the same time make a wallet or pouch in which to carry food and other essentials. From scabbards, attached to the belt on either side, hung a tomahawk and knife. The pants were either made of skins or homespun. Leggins and moccasins, made of leather and sewed with strips of deer skin, protected legs and feet. Lighter clothing, made in same fashion out of homespun or linsey, was worn in the warmer months. During the winter the summer clothing was worn under the skin garments for extra warmth. Caps were made of animal skins; hats of beaver hides or pressed animal hair.

These are the Americans that arose to the need of the hour. Needing a government, they organized the Watauga Association and administered it. This was the first organized political body, free and independent of any other state, in America. When their freedom was threatened they came out of the hills to fight. They had no staff, quartermaster, commissary, surgeon, or chaplain. A shot pouch, tomahawk, knife, powderhorn, knapsack, blanket and rifle constituted his outfit. The earth was his bed, the sky his cover, the creeks and rivers his source of water.

These are the soldiers that made up the unknown army that defeated Colonel Ferguson on King's Mountain, October 7th, 1780. The British timetable was broken, the Tories were frightened and Patriots were given time to reorganize. This is why King's Mountain is important in America's Revolutionary War history.

THE WAR IN REVIEW

Monument to the Signers of the Mecklenburg Declaration at Charlotte, North Carolina.

The King's Mountain victory signaled the turning point of the Revolutionary War in the South. After six long years of conflict, the fortunes of the Patriots hung in the balance. Nothing but faith and hope sustained the American cause during this dismal war. From the first battle at Lexington to the surrender of Cornwallis at Yorktown, it was a desperate fight. Congress had little power and less credit. Inadequate leadership and treachery from the inside were almost fatal.

Among the events that led up to the war with England were: The Stamp Act; the Riot in New York; The Boston Massacre; the Battle of Alamance; the Tea Parties; the Five Intolerable Acts imposed by England to punish Massachusetts; and the Taxation Without Representation. Instead of subduing the Patriots, these unjust acts and levies pushed them further away from the mother country. When the final breaking point came, many of the colonies pulled away and set up their own government. Virginia was the first. Others soon followed. They elected representatives who formed the first Continental Congress. This body met in Philadelphia on September 5, 1774.

The battles at Lexington and Concord during April 1775; the Mecklenburg Declaration of Independence at Charlotte, May 20th; the capture of Ticonderoga and Crown Point by Ethan Allen and the Green Mountain Boys, also in May; and the battle of Bunker Hill in June, were the opening guns of the long seven-years war that was destined to change the history of the world.

Patriots in every colony made ready to fight. Militia companies were formed in every settlement. They collected arms and ammunition and hid them in places of rendezvous.

The British placed General Gage in command, and sent in troops and naval reinforcements to put down the rebellion. The charter of Massachusetts was annulled — the port of Boston closed. The war had begun.

Ethan Allen and the Green Mountain Boys Capture Fort Ticonderoga

On July 3, 1775, General George Washington assumed command of the American Armies. He was hampered throughout the war with insufficient troops, desertions, and discontent. Unconquerable faith supported him throughout those dreary, desolate years. Integrity of purpose, and his understanding of the attitudes and prejudices of the people, aided him in uniting them in the objectives of their venture. Washington himself was the embodiment of the cause of freedom. His unselfish loyalty forced upon the people the realization that they and the new America were one. He reflected the true idealism of the Union and the Patriot.

George Washington takes command of the American Armies.

When Virginia revolted, Governor Dunmore fled to the safety of a British warship and attempted to wage war on the Virginia Colony from this vantage point. His force was badly defeated December 9th in the Battle of the Great Bridge. In retaliation, Dunmore caused the town of Norfolk to be burned New Year's Day, 1776. As active resistance spread, the Royal Governors from New Hampshire to Georgia fled to the safety of the British Navy. The King's Government collapsed and the Whigs took over, setting up their own Provincial Assemblies. They drilled and armed local companies of minutemen. Paper money was issued. Conditions were moving fast forward declaring independence.

The Americans who opposed the King called themselves ''Whigs''. The name was taken from the Liberal Party of England. This group had long opposed the conservative ''Tory'' element or Party. The Patriots adopted this name and became known as the party that supported the revolt.

Those who supported the King's cause were called ''Tories''. The colonists who adhered to this belief composed about one-third of the population in the new country. They fell into several classes. One was the sect that opposed war of any nature. Another segment, unfamiliar with the issues at stake, was satisfied

with existing conditions. They felt that England would soon subdue the Rebels and so preferred not to get involved.

The worst of the lot was that group of Tories, existing in every community, who made the name hated. Their whole effort in the war was for selfish, personal gain; and they saw in the conflict a possible way of acquiring their neighbors' property with legal sanction. They did not mind the killing, robbing, and plundering required to gain their objective. They visualized the rich reward for their faithfulness to the Crown. They turned from seemingly honest men to criminals, and they would betray a neighbor who had been their friend. They were much more dangerous than the armies in the battlefields.

The British used the Tories as they did the Indians. When they were through with them, they forsook these allies and left them homeless, friendless and without help. They literally turned their backs on them because they despised them. Many of the generous Americans helped their treacherous neighbors many times after the war was over. The Revolutionary War would have been over two or three years earlier but for this group of Tories.

A North Carolina Whig

With the Tory element stronger in the South, the British command made plans for a campaign in that direction. Governors Martin, of North Carolina, and Campbell, of South Carolina, thought the subjection of these two states would be a simple matter. Both had fled the colonies for the safety of a British warship, and together they planned a coastal invasion. A Highland Scottish settlement along Cross Creek (now Fayetteville, North Carolina), loyal to the Crown, answered Martin's appeal. The Scotchmen assembled some two thousand strong under General Donald McDonald, and marched to join Clinton on the coast. Learning this, the Patriots met the Tories at Moore's Creek Bridge February 27, 1776, and completely defeated the kilted force. The rebel forces in Eastern North Carolina were under the commands of Colonels James Moore, Alexander Lillington and Richard Caswell. Clinton, unable to land his force, withdrew.

Moore's Creek Battleground

For several months, General Washington had confined the English Army under General Howe, who had replaced General Gage, in Boston. Unable to make a direct assault because of a shortage of ammunition, Washington resorted to subterfuge. Howe, thinking he was outmanned, evacuated Boston on March 27th. He left behind a great amount of military supplies which were quickly taken over by the Americans. In addition, much needed food, left behind by the British, was also appropriated.

During this campaign, the first American flag was flown — the Grand Union. It contained thirteen stripes — seven red and six white — representing the thirteen colonies. The white cross of Saint Andrew and the red cross of Saint George were shifted to the upper lefthand corner of the staff. This indicated that the colonists had not yet declared independence. John Paul Jones first flew this flag from his battleship, December 3, 1775. Previously the British ensign had been flown in the colonies.

The next move of the British was against Charleston, South Carolina. General Clinton and Colonel Cornwallis with a strong command, and the support of a fleet of forty warships under Admiral Peter Parker, attacked the Palmetto Log Fort on Sullivan Island, June 28th, 1776. This fort was commanded by Colonel William Moultrie and four hundred thirty-five men. Isaac Motte and Francis Marion were his first and second officers. The British fired their three hundred cannons all day with little effect. Most of the shots would sink harmlessly into the soft logs or sand. The Americans, with only twenty-eight rounds of ammunition for their thirty cannons, had to make every shot count. Moultrie had instructed his gunners to wait until the gun smoke cleared from the British ships, then take careful aim before firing. The Bristol, Flag Ship of Admiral Parker, was hit on the quarter-deck. Governor William Campbell, Admiral Parker and Captain Morris were all severely wounded. Over two hundred Tars were killed and wounded during the contest. Several ships went aground, and one blew up when a Patriot shot hit her powder storeroom. At sundown, the crippled British Fleet retired without doing any significant damage to Charleston and its valiant defenders. Why no move was made by three thousand regulars who were landed on Long Island, has always been a mystery.

Lord Clinton

Sergeant Jasper rescues Flag at Fort Moultrie.

Colonel Moultrie had placed a regiment of sharpshooters, under Colonel Isaac Huger, on James Island. These men in rifle pits were his second line of defense. Among the men of this force was a platoon of Overmountain men under Lieutenant Felix Walker. During the day of the battle, the citizens of Charleston watched the progress of the fight from vantage points, including house tops. They knew their safety and welfare depended on those determined perspiring men in Fort Sullivan.

Colonel Moultrie was flying a beautiful flag over the Fort. It was blue with a white crescent, and the motto LIBERTY was emblazoned across its length.

During the battle, a shot from one of the British guns cut the flag staff, and it fell outside the Fort wall, on the battle side. Sergeant Jasper, seemingly unafraid of the shots flying all around, clambered down and regained the flag. Back inside the Fort wall, using a halberd or sponge stick for a staff, Jasper soon had the flag flying over the Fort again. A big cheer was raised by the watching populace for this brave performance, and Governor Rutledge awarded Sergeant Jasper a sword in recognition of his valor. Jasper accepted the sword but refused a Lieutenant's commission. He was killed in a later battle.

Colonel Moultrie had eleven men killed and twenty-six wounded. Some historians have rated this battle as one of the three decisive victories of the Revolution. The Moore's Creek and Fort Moutltrie victories saved the South from invasion for some two years.

On July 2, 1776, Richard Henry Lee made a motion in Congress that the "united colonies are, and of a right ought to be, free and independent states." To give form to this motion, Congress adopted on July 4th, "The Declaration of Independence," written by Thomas Jefferson of Virginia. This paper is perhaps the most important political instrument ever written. By its virtue, each colony became a state.

Among the many events of the year 1776 was the Cherokee Uprising against the Overmountain men; the Battle of Long Island; the loss of New York to the British; the defeats at White Plains and in Canada; the destruction of the Lake Champlain Fleet; the British recapture of Crown Point and Newport, Rhode Island; and Washington's surprise victory over the Hessians in Trenton on Christmas Day. Thus the historic year of 1776 was a gloomy one, despite victories at Princeton, Bennington, Stillwater and Saratoga. Losses at Brandywine and Germantown brought into the open the animosity of some of the command toward Washington. Several members of Congress were loud in their clamor against Washington's conduct of the war. They wanted him to drive the enemy from Philadelphia immediately. But General Washington, knowing how weak his army was, did not dare let the enemy know his weakness.

A plot by a French officer, General Conway, assisted by Gates and many other jealous officers, made a desperate attempt to discredit Washington and place Gates as Commander-in-Chief. The victory at Saratoga was cited as a comparison of their ability. Gates never gave credit to the small companies, led by their individual commanders, that won Saratoga. Gates wanted to retreat. It was men like Daniel Morgan who saved the day. Gates lied out of the situation; Conway resigned and apologized. Washington was too well respected and loved for the loyal members of Congress to do anything as foolish as replace him. This was known as "the Conway Cabal."

Burgoyne surrenders to Gates after Saratoga.

Winter at Valley Forge

On November 15 "The Articles of Confederation," providing a form of government for the United States, was adopted by Congress; but these did not go into effect until after the war because the thirteen colonies had to ratify the document.

The winter at Valley Forge can well be called the Valley of Despair. This moral scar on American political history was a direct result of jealousy, corruption and duplicity. Many of the congressmen, and some of the highly-ranked military officers, were jealous of George Washington and his loyal command. They were willing to do anything to hurt the General.

Even though it was a minority group, their selfish acts brought a period of desperation to the fighting Patriots of America. Using bribery in the right places, these traitors had wormed their way into responsible positions. They filled their own pockets, while handling government supplies and contracts. Frequently they sold the supplies, intended for our troops, to the British for higher prices. Sometimes they would destroy food, clothing and other supplies rather than accept the paper money issued by the government. Many of the appointed commissary officers would let food, clothing and tents rot in barrels on road sides, if they could not see a profit for themselves. The suffering at Valley Forge and other sections meant nothing to these mercenaries.

Soldiers at Valley Forge went hungry, shoeless, blanketless, and many shelterless because of this situation. General Washington had caused many shelters to be built from the trees of the area, but not near enough could be put up before the winter storms had made such work impossible. Soldiers often had to share one ragged suit between them. Valley Forge will always be a symbol of American patriotism at its noblest and purest form.

Then came spring and a pledge of help from France. With this turn of events, new recruits swelled Washington's force. General Clinton, who had succeeded Howe, evacuated Philadelphia. Washington followed and attacked Clinton near Monmouth, New Jersey June 28, 1778. Clinton continued his retreat to New York. The American Army set up camp at White Plains, pinning Clinton's forces to the seaboard.

Meanwhile, the Tories and Indians were invading the Wyoming Valley of Pennsylvania, plundering, burning and killing. At night, these invaders would torture their prisoners with savage devices. They followed this destruction of homes and settlements on through Cherry Valley located in New York State. This savage Tory-Indian force was led by Colonel John Butler. In all sections of the country, such warfare was carried on by some of the Tories and Indian renegades. This savage and useless cruelty hurt the King's cause. It created a lasting hostility in the hearts of the Americans in all thirteen States. The Indian's alliance with England became a tragic affair for them.

NORTHWESTERN CAMPAIGN

British Agents in the southwest and northwest territories, were busy inciting the Indians to attack the frontier settlements of Tennessee and Kentucky. In the northwest, the English had posted garrisons at Kaskaskia on the Mississippi; Cahokia, across the river from St. Louis; Vincennes on the Wabash; and Fort Detroit on Lake Erie. Colonel George Rogers Clarke secured backing and authority from Patrick Henry, Governor of Virginia, for a

Indian Massacre from McGee History by Victor Perard

campaign into the northwest territory. Captains Joseph Bowman, Leonard Helm, William Harrod and Major William B. Smith were commissioned to enlist several companies from the Kentucky and Holston Settlements. The place of muster was the Falls of the Ohio. Colonel Clarke found a much smaller force than he expected. When the type and extent of the proposed campaign was revealed to the enlisted men, desertions were many.

George Rogers Clarke

Undaunted, Colonel Clarke captured Kaskaskia July 4, 1778, without bloodshed. Shortly afterward, Vincennes was occupied in like manner. Colonel Henry Hamilton, Lieutenant Governor of Canada, regained possession of the Garrison at Vincennes, December 1778. With a force of one hundred thirty men, Colonel Clarke set out to attack Vincennes. The Patriot force had to travel through miles of rough country, often crossing icy streams waist deep. They recaptured Vincennes on February 23, 1779. Colonel Henry Hamilton, called the hair (scalp) buyer, was captured, along with his force and a big store of supplies intended for the Indians. Colonel Clarke's conquest of the northwest saved that territory for America. Without this successful undertaking, the Canadian line could well have been the Ohio River, instead of being along the Great Lakes.

Another campaign of equal importance to the Tennessee settlers was the Chickamauga Campaign, commanded by Colonel Evan Shelby. Some six hundred men embarked on boats from the mouth of Big Creek on the Holston River in April 1779. The streams, swollen by spring freshets, made for a fast trip to the Chickamauga towns. The surprise attack on this Indian country was a complete success. The Indians fled to the hills and forests. Large stores of supplies, furnished by the English for the attack on the Tennessee settlers, were captured. Many of the towns were burned.

Captain John Montgomery, sent to the northwest with Colonel Clarke, was with this force at the capture of Kaskaskia. Captain Montgomery was sent back to the Holston Settlements to recruit more troops. During the winter months of 1778-1779, Captain Montgomery had enlisted one hundred fifty men for a year's service. Colonel Shelby, planning the Chickamauga Campaign and needing more men, asked the aid of this force. Governor Patrick Henry ordered Captain Montgomery and his men to participate with Shelby. At the close of this mission, Captain Montgomery and his men continued the trip by boat. They rejoined Colonel Clarke in the northwest. Montgomery, promoted to Colonel, was placed in charge of the Kaskaskia district for a period. Captain James Shelby, son of Colonel Evan Shelby, accompanied Colonel Montgomery with sixteen men. Captain Shelby was placed in command of Fort Patrick Henry at Vincennes.

These two campaigns stopped, for the time being, the large-scale Indian attacks on the settlers of Tennessee and Kentucky, as planned by the English agents. These two ventures proved most important in the course of events that followed.

Montgomery County in Tennessee was named for Colonel Montgomery. The county seat was named Clarkesville in honor of Colonel George Rogers Clarke.

THE WAR MOVES SOUTH

General George Washington, unable to obtain sufficient money or supplies for an active campaign, determined to contain General Clinton to the seaboard. Because of the short term enlistments and shortage of supplies, the American force had again dwindled to less than five thousand men. A month's pay would barely purchase one good meal, and better clothing could be had at home. The American currency was almost worthless, and Congress did not have sufficient influence and strength to make a move.

General Clinton, having failed in the campaign against the northern states, turned his attention again toward the South. He sent Colonel Campbell with three thousand troops to attack Savannah, Georgia. He soon proceeded to overrun and plunder Georgia. Pleased with this foothold, Clinton sailed south to personally

THE SIEGE OF CHARLESTON.
After the picture by Chappel.

direct the campaign. With a strong fleet and an army of thirteen thousand, Clinton laid siege to Charleston. Two months later, on May 12, 1780, General Lincoln surrendered. Lincoln never had sufficient supplies or troops to withstand a siege. When the British entered Charleston, they, with their Hessian mercenaries, pillaged the city. The homes of the Patriots were taken over or burned. Property was taken from any person thought to have anti-royalist sentiments. South Carolina suffered more than any other state during the Revolutionary War.

General Clinton, quickly taking advantage of the defeat of Lincoln's army at Charleston, sent British detachments in all directions. He wanted to subdue the Patriots and demonstrate to the people that it was much better to take the oath of allegiance than to fight. Placing General Cornwallis in charge, with instructions to finish off South Carolina and then move on into North Carolina and Virginia, Clinton returned to New York.

The British and Prussian officers were more interested in filling their own pockets than reuniting the Empire. Thus, the Whigs of the southland faced loss of life, family, property and possessions in the savage raping, wholesale ransacking and reign of terror that followed.

Colonel Abraham Buford and four hundred Virginians, arriving too late to assist Colonel Lincoln in the defense of Charleston, had turned and started back toward North Carolina. Colonel Banastre Tarleton was sent in pursuit and overtook them near Waxhaw, South Carolina. When Colonel Buford saw the hopelessness of the battle, he asked for quarter for his men. Tarleton, wanting to make them an example for the rest of the South, cut them down without mercy or regard of their surrender request. One hundred thirteen were killed outright. Fifty were cut and maimed so badly that they could not be moved. Only fifty-three men were taken prisoners. Less that two hundred were able to escape. This was the type of butchery practiced by Tarleton and his dragoons. The battle cry of the South became "REMEMBER BUFORD AND HIS QUARTERS".

Tarleton's massacre of the Buford Company at Waxhaw, South Carolina

Thomas Sumpter

Francis Marion

Andrew Pickens

But the South was not that easily taken. Small partisan groups, under leaders chosen from their own members, made fringe war on the English. They would plough by day and fight by night. This type of warfare slowed up the British in their Southern campaign. Among the outstanding leaders were Francis Marion, Thomas Sumpter, Andrew Pickens, Elijah Clarke, Charles McDowell, Andrew Hampton, Benjamin Cleveland, Joseph Winston and many others. Congress finally sent help. A sizeable force under General Gates, who was appointed to take Lincoln's place, composed of various militia groups, was assembled. Two thousand men came from Delaware and Maryland, and they were joined by several companies of militia from Virginia and North Carolina. Gates had been appointed Commander-in-chief by Congress, against Washington's advice. Gates took charge in midsummer at Hillsborough. General Richard Caswell, appointed by the assembly as Major General of the North Carolina militia, joined Gates' force with his command.

In August, Gates moved his army into South Carolina to meet Cornwallis. On the night of August 16th, the advance guards of both armies stumbled into each other. A sharp exchange of shots occurred. Both generals waited until daybreak to give battle. At first dawn, Cornwallis ordered his men to charge. Gates, a poor general, muddled his plans, lost his head and fled. His men, leaderless and demoralized, fled in every direction. The entire army was either killed, captured or scattered. Gates himself did not stop, except for food and sleep, until he

Gates Defeat at Camden   by Chappel

reached Hillsborough some 200 miles away. The result of this battle proved nearly disastrous to the southern patriots. To the British and Tories it seemed to signal final success.

Colonel Patrick Ferguson, aide to Cornwallis, was sent into the district of Ninety-Six to fortify that garrison and organize the Tories. After arriving with a force of some 200 men, Ferguson made this garrison his headquarters. He had the British Mandate read to the people of that section: "We come not to make war on women and children but to relieve their distress." This sounded good to the Tory-inclined. They flocked to the British standard in large numbers. Companies and regiments were organized. Fort Ninety-Six was so named because it was ninety-six miles from the Indian town of Keowee, located just across the river from Fort Prince Charles. Prince Charles was near Keowee River, some ten miles south of the North Carolina line.

The new Tory recruits were thoroughly drilled and disciplined by Ferguson's staff. Small detachments were sent into the surrounding country to recruit others and obtain supplies. These platoons were also on the hunt for Whigs. This instituted a reign of terror in South Carolina and Georgia. Troops under Major Dunlap and Lieutenant Taylor ransacked, plundered, burned and killed. Horses were turned loose on fields

Elijah Clarke

of grain that belonged to the Patriots. Homes were burned, forcing mothers and children to find shelter and food in the forests as best they could. Patriots were shot just because a jealous Tory neighbor had turned their names over to the British leaders.

In Georgia, Colonel Elijah Clarke, commander of a partisan force of the Augusta area, felt forced to disband his company. He and his men decided to wait until more favorable circumstances allowed for renewed fighting against the British. Colonel Clarke, an active patriot leader, figured prominently in the action that took place during the following weeks and months. One of his officers, Colonel John Jones, and some thirty-five recruits, decided to travel north and join the Carolinians. John Freeman was one of the officers, and Benjamin Lawrence served as guide.

They palmed themselves off as Tory recruits enroute to join Ferguson. In the present Greenville, South Carolina, area they heard of the Cedar Springs engagement, and asked to be directed to the defeated Tory detachment, that they might join them in their attempt to regain prisoners taken. A Tory guide volunteered this service. On reaching the Tory encampment about midnight, Colonel Jones surrounded the sleeping soldiers and captured them all. The Tory guide did not know what was taking place until it was too late. The next morning Jones released the prisoners on parole. The captured supplies, ammunition, and guns outfitted his small company; and taking the Tory horses, they forced the unwilling guide to lead them to McDowell's camp.

Fort Prince Charles was located on the east bank of the Keowee River. Colonel Innes, commander of this post, was unaware of the presence of the McDowell force in the area. Innes sent Majors Dunlap and Mills, with a sizeable company, to pursue and capture Colonel Jones and his company of Georgians. Dunlap located the Patriot camp and, thinking he was attacking Jones' small company, charged across the Pacolet River into the unsuspecting Camp of Colonel Charles McDowell. A warning shot by one sentry enabled the Americans to fire on Dunlap's men. Realizing his mistake, Dunlap withdrew across the river. Colonel Andrew Hampton's son Noah was killed in this action, and Hampton blamed McDowell for not putting out more sentries. This was one of three successive night fights: the Cedar Springs attack on Colonel Thomas; Jones' attack on the loyalist camp; and the attack on McDowell by Dunlap and Mills.

McDowell, convinced that Ferguson's invasion threatened the settlements of Western North Carolina, sent for help across the mountains. Messages were sent to Colonel John Sevier and Colonel Isaac Shelby. Sevier had lost his wife, Sarah Hawkins Sevier, in February and could not leave at the time. Also he was unwilling to leave the frontier exposed to Indian attack. Sevier did arrange to send part of his regiment under the command of Major Charles Robertson. Colonel Shelby, delayed because of business in Kentucky, joined McDowell in July with two hundred riflemen. Colonel Shelby was placed in charge of the Overmountain men. About the same time, Colonel Clarke arrived in the area with a company of Georgians. He was looking for the McDowell force but found Sumpter instead.

Fort Anderson, located on Thicketty Creek and commanded by Captain Moore, was headquarters for bands of plundering Tories. Colonel Sumpter directed Clarke to join with Shelby, Robertson, and Hampton for a surprise attack on this Fort. About six hundred mounted riflemen started at sunset and journeyed some twenty-five miles to the Fort which they surrounded at daybreak. Colonel Shelby sent Captain William Cocke to make a demand for the surrender of the stockade. Moore replied that he would defend it to the last man.

Shelby then withdrew and told his officers his plans. He circled the Fort with his men in shooting distance, making ready the attack. This force made such a formidable showing that Moore surrendered without a shot. Ninety-three Loyalists were taken. The Patriots captured two hundred fifty stands of arms and a large store of supplies and ammunition.

Carrying the supplies and prisoners, Shelby and his men returned to headquarters at McDowell's camp. The McDowell force now numbered 1000; Ferguson's between 1500 and 2000. The Carolina Patriots maintaining camp at Cherokee Ford sent small detachments to harass British troops who were traveling through the countryside enlisting and collecting supplies. Ferguson made several attempts to surprise these groups, but the ever-watchful Americans were never there when the British arrived. They had no fixed camp and were constantly on the move.

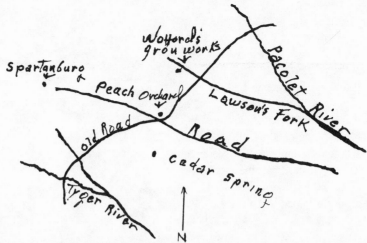

On August 7th, Shelby and his men stopped to rest, eat and feed their horses near Fair Forest Creek. Scouts reported the enemy to be one-half mile away. One of Dunlap's Tories accidently fired a gun which warned Shelby's men of the nearness of the British. The Americans withdrew toward the Old Iron Works near Lawson's Ford on the Pacolet and took their positions near Cedar Springs on ground suitable for battle. Major Dunlap soon made his appearance, confident of victory. The severely-fought battle lasted about half an hour. Dunlap's Tory militia waged a terrific fight, but Shelby's and Clarke's well-placed riflemen inflicted heavy losses. Many hand fights occurred during this battle. One was between Colonel Clarke and two Tories. Being a giant of a man, he soon knocked one down and the other fled. The Americans beat back the enemy with heavy losses. Dunlap's fleeing forces came up with Ferguson's main force some two miles from Cedar Springs. The retreating men were reorganized, and the Tories advanced to give battle to the Patriots. Shelby and Clarke meanwhile began a withdrawing, delaying type of action. After several miles of this, Ferguson abandoned the chase.

McDowell, fearing an attack on his camp at Cherokee, moved to Smith's Ford, about ten miles farther south. Colonels Clarke and Shelby remained in camp several days, letting their men get a much needed rest. Several needed to have their wounds treated, and time to mend. Clarke, his son, and Major Charles Robertson were slightly wounded during this battle. The location of this battle site has been much contested. Suffice to say that it was near Cedar Springs or Wofford's Iron Works.

MUSGROVE MILL BATTLE

Scouts reported that two hundred men were stationed at Musgrove's Mill, forty miles from McDowell's Camp. These loyalist troops were placed there to guard the ford across Enoree River. Ferguson was camped about midway between the American camp and Musgrove's Mill. Since Shelby's and Robertson's time of enlistment was about up, they volunteered for this assignment. Colonel Elijah Clarke and his Georgians also asked to take part in the mission. With three hundred mounted riflemen they set out in the late afternoon. They wanted to make most of the trip during the night. This was done for two reasons: secrecy and speed. A night march in August was favorable to the stamina of horses. They also had to slip unobserved past Ferguson's force. They followed a road part of the way, sacrificing possible detection for speed. Among the officers were Captains James McCall, Samuel Hammond, James Williams, Joseph McDowell, Valentine Sevier, and David Vance.

13

Among the streams crossed on their route were the Pacolet, and Tyger. They passed within four miles of Ferguson's camp, in the Brandon Settlement, and rode all night without stopping. The Americans halted about one mile from Musgrove's Mill and sent scouts to reconnoiter. The scouts ran into a small detachment of Tory scouts returning to camp. In the exchange of shots, two of the Loyalists were killed and others wounded. The Americans, though some were wounded, were able to ride back to the main force. A native Patriot living nearby informed the Americans that several hundred reinforcements had arrived the night before from Fort Ninety-Six, enroute to join Ferguson.

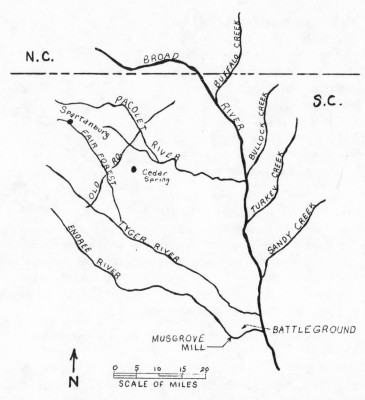

The news of the larger force made a desperate situation for the Mountaineers. The men were weary and their horses were tired because of the long night march of forty miles. But Ferguson, being stationed at their rear, left little room for retreat. They had no choice but to fight. On a timbered ridge about one-half mile from the mill, an improvised breastwork of logs and brush was thrown together. A fence offered some protection. The American lines extended some three hundred yards in a semicircle along the ridge and across the road. The Patriots took their positions, somewhat concealed behind this cover. Shelby took the right wing, Clarke the left, Captain Williams the middle. A corps of twenty horsemen was placed behind each wing for reserves. Later, these came to be needed in the heat of battle.

Meanwhile the arrival of the two remaining Tory scouts at the mill caused much commotion. The Loyalist officers had their headquarters in Edmond Musgrove's home. A hurried council was held. Colonel Innes, in charge of the detachment moving to join Ferguson, was for attacking the rebels at once. Others contended for a delay until more information could be obtained. Colonel Innes prevailed. The British command organized their forces and made ready to catch the "scurvy ragamuffins," as they regarded the Americans. Leaving about one hundred men in camp as reserves, the loyalists crossed the river and advanced. Among the British officers were Major Frazier, in command of the regular detachment stationed at the ford; Captain Abraham De Peyster; Captain David Fanning, who had taken part in the battle of Alamance; and Colonel Daniel Clay, a famous Tory leader of the area.

The American commanders had improvised a plan which was effectively put into action. Captain Shadrack Innman was sent forward with twenty-five mounted men. His orders were to fire upon and provoke the enemy to cross the river and attack. After firing he was to retire, hoping to draw the British into the prepared trap. The strategy worked well. The loyalists eagerly followed, hoping to bayonet the lot. Captain Innman kept up a show of fighting and retreating. About two hundred yards from the mountaineer breastworks, the English formed lines and advanced. Their first shots went over the heads of the concealed Americans. The mountaineers held their fire as ordered. Their leaders had told them to wait until they could count the buttons on the British coats, then sight their object sure.

14

The British center, against whom Captain Innman made his feigned attack, saw him retire in apparent confusion. Pressing forward with beat of drum and sound of bugle, shouting "Huzza for King George," the British approached to within seventy yards of the improvised breastworks before the Americans met them with a deadly wall of fire. Their superiority in numbers enabled the Loyalists to continue the attack. A strong force, led by Colonel Innes and Frazier, charged Shelby's wing with bayonet and drove them back after a desperate struggle. Clarke sent his reserve to help Shelby. At this critical moment, Colonel Innes fell wounded. Shelby rallied his men, who raised a frontier Indian war yell and charged into the enemy, forcing them back. An attack against Clarke's wing failed to break that line. Many of the British officers fell during these forward charges, and the few that were left could not rally the men. The Americans now advanced from their positions, and with savage yells began chasing and slashing the fleeing militia. It was a melee.

The British-Tory troops were now in a panicked retreat, closely followed by the entire American force who were knocking down the enemy as they caught them. Captain Shadrack Innman was killed during this final charge. The moans and screams of the wounded and dying, and the pursuit of the retreating British by the Indian-yelling mountaineers, over a battlefield covered with a canopy of smoke, was soul shaking. The terrified Loyalists dropped everything and fled for their lives. Their one thought was to escape those yelling, savage devils at their rear.

Some of the British and Tory reserves had climbed on top of Musgrove's house to watch the fun, never doubting the outcome. They thought that the retreating rebel horsemen under Captain Innman constituted the entire American force in the vicinity. They had raised their voices in shouts of victory as the small force seemed to be retreating. Suddenly the whole picture changed! The onlookers were stunned by the tremendous burst of gunfire. The hidden Americans were mowing down the British in their chaotic retreat. Many of this group on the housetop were paroled Tories. They did not want any part of this savage horde. Long before the retreating Loyalists reached the ford, these men had grabbed their knapsacks and headed for Fort Ninety-Six.

The battle lasted about an hour. The remaining Loyalist force, under the command of Captain De Peyster, returned to Ninety-Six that day, fearing that the Americans might make another attack. Only a small detachment was left to bury the dead and care for the wounded.

Musgrove Battle Ridge

Bridge across Enoree River at site
of Musgrove's Mill

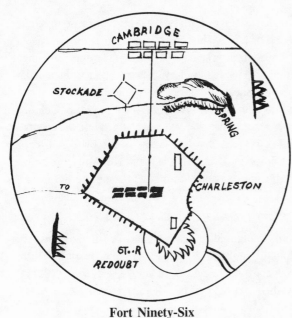

Fort Ninety-Six

The Americans captured around seventy prisoners. It is estimated that about half of the British force was either captured, killed, or wounded. A Tory scouting party arrived soon after the battle. Thinking they might recapture some of the prisoners, they charged across the river to attack the mountaineers, but these gentlemen had departed. On the American side, four were killed and ten wounded. This engagement is thought to have been one of the hardest fought battles with small arms, of any engagement during the southern phase of the Revolutionary War.

At the close of the battle, the mountaineers were anxious to take advantage of the victory, and to continue on to Fort Ninety-Six some twenty-five miles distant. Preparations were being made for such a move when Francis Jones, an express messenger from McDowell's camp, arrived with the news of General Gates' disastrous defeat at Camden. The letter was written by General Richard Caswell, a commanding officer under Gates. The letter, addressed to McDowell and all commanding officers, instructed them to get out of the way before they were cut off. Shelby recognized Caswell's handwriting and knew the news was authentic. McDowell also sent word that he was moving to the vicinity of Gilbert Town.

The situation of Shelby's and Clarke's forces was extremely bad. They were unable to return to McDowell's camp. Gates' southern army was defeated, captured, killed and scattered. The position of Sumpter's forces was unknown. In the rear were Cruger's trained regulars at Fort Ninety-Six, and Ferguson's army on their flank. The Overmountain men had but one choice—to run for their lives. The flush of victory changed to desperate retreat. They decided to take the backwoods route and rejoin McDowell at Gilbert Town. Each prisoner was placed in the charge of three Patriot riders, who were to alternate in carrying him on their horses, and each prisoner carried his gun minus flint. In a short time the entire force was moving, knowing that Ferguson would soon be on their trail in an effort to overtake them.

The mountaineers, burdened with their prisoners, traveled as rapidly as possible toward the northwest and the mountains, leaving Ferguson's position to the right. As expected, a strong detachment of Ferguson's men was in pursuit. Under Colonel Shelby's energetic urging, the wearied men traveled mile after mile with no rest except to water their horses. They ate raw corn snatched from the fields as they rode and now and then, a peach plucked from the trees as they passed under them. During that day and night the mountaineers rode sixty miles from the battlefield. In the course of two nights and one day, these hardy men had traveled one hundred miles on horseback, and fought a battle. All this was done without any food, sleep or rest during hot August weather. Ferguson's men gave up the chase after forty miles. The Americans, with their prisoners, finally reached McDowell's force at Gilbert Town.

The detachment from Ferguson's force came near catching the mountaineers; they came within thirty minutes of the tired Patriots. After locating the spot where the fleeing Americans had stopped to water their horses, they gave up the chase. Their own mounts near exhaustion, and not knowing how far ahead the enemy, they decided to turn back.

The tired men, faces and eyes swollen, kept pushing on to safety. They did not know that Ferguson's men had turned back. Musgrove's Mill Battle and the Musgrove Family are traditional stories that few people outside of South Carolina have taken time to read.

As the leaders rested in camp, they reviewed the events of the past weeks and months. They knew that Ferguson would move up into the western section of South Carolina and North Carolina looking for supplies. They explored the prospect of organizing a volunteer force large enough to cope with the growing Loyalist army. All of the officers and men discussed such a plan and agreed to participate in its execution. These talks were very informal, but it was here that the King's Mountain campaign was born. Colonel Charles McDowell agreed to send word to Colonel Benjamin Cleveland, commander of the Wilkes County Tory fighters, and Major Joseph Winston, who headed a like force in Surry County. Messengers offered their services as "go-betweens" for the Overmountain men and the Patriots of McDowell and other partisan forces.

Restored home of Colonel David Vance, grandfather of Zebulon Vance, Civil War Governor of North Carolina. Many of the events recorded came from the papers of David Vance. He was active in many of the battles preceding King's Mountain.

Three brothers — James, Jack, and Archibald Neal — living in Turkey Cove volunteered to serve from the McDowell group. Colonel Cleveland, when advised of the plan, appointed his brother Robert Cleveland and Gideon Lewis as messengers to Sevier and Shelby. After a much needed rest, most of the volunteer groups returned to their own settlements.

Colonels McDowell and Hampton, with less than two hundred men, decided to remain in the vicinity of Gilbert Town. Soon they would be forced deeper into the mountains by the approach of Ferguson's army. Colonel Clarke and his men headed back toward their homes in the area of Augusta, Georgia. Clarke had hopes of accomplishing a move by an unexpected attack there. Colonel Hampton and Captain James Williams were designated to deliver the prisoners to the authorities at Hillsborough.

Governor Rutledge of South Carolina was at Hillsborough, and Captain Williams, in making his report, conveyed the idea that he, Williams, was in general command during the battle at Musgrove's Mill and was responsible for the victory. He gave Colonels Shelby and Clarke very little credit. As a result of this report, Governor Rutledge gave Williams the rank of Brigadier-General.

Ferguson's move into Western North Carolina forced the small partisan groups deeper into the hills. Tories of this section were flocking to the King's standard. They thought the British were absolute victors. With

Recruiting Tories

the fall of Charleston; the massacre of Buford's men; the total route of Gates' army at Camden; the defeat of Sumpter's force at the mouth of Fishing Creek by Tarleton, a cloud of gloom hung over the country.

Colonel Ferguson, hoping to break up the McDowell-Hampton force, made a surprise attack against them on Bedford's Hill. The engagement, an indecisive one, was bitterly contested by the greatly outnumbered mountaineers. They fought the Loyalists Indian-style and inflicted heavy damage. Major Dunlap of Ninety-Six was wounded during this battle. The Tories suffered such heavy casualties they withdrew.

THE OVERMOUNTAIN PEOPLE

It was near Watauga River between Gap Creek and Buffalo Creek that McDowell's people built their temporary camp. This location is also near Sycamore Shoals and site of Fort Caswell.

Colonel Charles McDowell and Colonel Andrew Hampton, realizing the impossibility of opposing Ferguson with their small force, led one hundred sixty men across the mountains to the Watauga Settlement. The men built crude huts and lean-tos along the Watauga River, near the mouths of Gap and Buffalo Creeks. The people of the community made sure they had sufficient supplies. McDowell told the Overmountain people of the high-handed methods and destruction of Ferguson. Some of the men left on the other side of the mountains had driven their stock deep into the mountain gorges and caves, in an effort to save their limited supply. Many of the men moved their entire families across the mountains. A few of the men left behind were instructed to take the oath under Ferguson in order to save stock, homes and people.

The plight of the Patriots is summed up in a quotation from Theodore Roosevelt's "Winning the West": "Except for occasional small guerilla parties, there was not a single organized body of American troops left south of Gates' broken and dispirited army. All the southern lands lay at the feet of the conquerors. The British leaders, overbearing and arrogant, held almost unchecked sway throughout the Carolinas and Georgia; and looking northward they made ready for the conquest of Virginia. Their right flank was covered by the waters of the ocean, their left by the high mountain barrier-chains, beyond which stretched the intermidable forest; and they had as little thought of danger from one side as the other."

So desperate was the situation, that many of the people were willing to just let the British have Georgia and the Carolinas without a struggle. Why fight against such losing odds? Liberty meant nothing to people of this make-up.

South Carolina Governor John Rutledge was conducting whatever state business he could from Hillsborough, North Carolina. For about three years there was no constituted government in that state. Civil war was rampant. Tories and Whigs were fighting almost constantly. South Carolina furnished more men and money than any other state during the Revolution. It also suffered more. It is said that in the District of Ninety-Six no less than thirty battles were fought. After the war, some fourteen hundred widows and orphans were listed in that area alone.

From Williams' **Tennessee During the Revolution,** we copy a letter from Governor Rutledge, written September 20, 1780.

"Not a man from Virginia is in this State, except about 250 Continentals under Beaufort (Buford), and about sixty of the militia who ran away from the action with Cornwallis, and who have lately been brought to Hillsborough; nor can we hear of any being on the march from Virginia.....Alas! When may we really and reasonably expect that all those things will come to pass."

Gloom and despair prevailed over most of the South. No help was available from General Washington. He had no troops he could spare. State treasuries were exhausted. Many of the partisan groups had to depend on clothing, weapons and ammunition from a slain enemy or a fallen comrade. Often a man without a gun would stay in the background until a weapon was available in this way.

Governor Rutledge of South Carolina

FERGUSON'S THREAT

Colonel Ferguson was riding high with his successful campaign. An energetic officer, he was seeing a victorius end to the war in the South. Visions of a rich reward, as one of the successful conquerors, no doubt filled his mind. Little did he realize that these were false illusions, soon to be destroyed. His mind kept reminding him of the hated backwater men. Those Indian-yelling, bushwacking Overmountain men had been a thorn in his flesh too long. Colonel De Peyster, who had in the meanwhile joined his command, had

**Ferguson's Headquarters
at Gilbert Town**

evidently reported that it was those Indian-yelling mountaineers, that had wrought such havoc at Musgrove's Mill. Ferguson became angry every time he thought of their successes at Pacolet, Thicketty Fort, Wofford's Iron Works, and the worst of all at Musgrove's Mill. He decided to do something about it.

Samuel Phillips, a prisoner of war in the Tory camp, was a distant cousin of Shelby and lived in the Holston settlement. Ferguson, thinking to throw a scare into those uncouth barbarians from the Overmountain country, wrote a message to Shelby and the other leaders. He sent a message by Phillips; Ferguson did not know it but this message proved to be his death warrant. The message read in effect: if he, Shelby, and the other backwater leaders did not desist from their opposition to the British Arms, he would march his army over the mountains, hang their leaders, and lay waste the country with fire and sword.

Colonel Isaac Shelby, upon receipt of this message and having questioned Phillips regarding Ferguson's location and strength, immediately saddled his horse and rode some forty miles to the home of Colonel John Sevier near the Nolichucky River. Sevier had recently married Catherine Sherrill (the Bonnie Kate of Tennessee); and the Seviers were in the midst of a big festival gathering. Neighbors and friends from far and near were present. Horse racing, a barbecue and dancing were in full sway. Upon learning the seriousness of Shelby's visit, the two men withdrew from the crowd and began a three-day conference. The plan, discussed earlier by Shelby, McDowell, Clarke and Robertson, was explored. They canvassed the possible number of men they could muster, and how to finance the campaign. Would the Virginians under Colonel William Campbell and Colonel Arthur Campbell help?

The Pioneer

Old Tilson Water Mill built in the 1840's

19

Colonel Isaac Shelby: prominent in the early settlement of Tennessee, Indian campaigns, and politics; commanded forces at Thicketty Creek, Cedar Springs, and Musgrove's Mill; declined President Monroe's appointment as Secretary of War; first Governor of Kentucky.

Isaac Shelby

Colonel John Sevier: Clerk and Magistrate, Watauga Association; defender at Fort Caswell, 1776; Clerk of Washington County Court; Colonel of Militia; Governor, State of Franklin; first elected Governor of Tennessee.

John Sevier

A PIONEER MUSTER

September 25th was the date set for the muster at Sycamore Shoals (Elizabethton, Tennessee). Both men sent riders over the countryside to call in their men. Money for the undertaking was secured from John Adair, entry taker for Sullivan County. Adair told the two men, Sevier and Shelby: "I have no authority by law to make that disposition of this money; it belongs to the impoverished State of North Carolina, and I dare not appropriate a cent of it to any other purpose; but if the country is overrun by the British, our liberty is gone. Let the money go too. Take it, if the enemy, by its use, is driven from the country. I can trust that country to justify and vindicate my conduct, so take it." John Sevier and Isaac Shelby gave their personal pledges for its return, should the State of North Carolina so demand. (Adair was given a receipt for its use by North Carolina in 1782.)

The grist mills of Baptist McNabb and Mathew Talbot were busy grinding corn for bread making. The women busied themselves with their looms and needles, making and mending clothes for their menfolk. Mrs. John Sevier spent her honeymoon making suits for the Colonel and his sons. Mary Patton supervised one of the powder mills. Lead for bullets was mined from a hill near the Nolichucky River, in the present Bumpass Cove section of Unicoi County. Every hand turned out to help in the defense of home and country.

On the appointed day, the whole countryside seemed to be gathering for the muster. Most of the men were accompanied by their families. Beef cattle for meat were driven to Sycamore Shoals. So many wanted to go that a draft had to be made. Sevier and Shelby knew that the frontiers were in constant danger from Indian raids, so the very young boys and older men were drafted to stay home to protect the women and children. It was some gathering, as the people arrived from every cove, valley and hillside. Mothers, sisters, sweethearts and children were present to see their menfolk off to battle. This would be the last farewell for some.

Two hundred forty men were selected from Sullivan County to follow Shelby; a like number from Washington County under Sevier. Some two hundred Virginians came with Colonel William Campbell. Colonel Arthur Campbell brought about two hundred more militia of his Virginia Command, and placed them under Colonel William Campbell's command. Already on the grounds were the troops of Colonel Charles McDowell and Colonel Andrew Hampton. Major Charles Robertson was left in charge of the Washington County forces to protect the frontier. Colonel Anthony Bledsoe was placed in command of the Sullivan home force.

On the morning of September 26th, the men gathered in companies, accompanied by their families for a religious service. Colonel Sevier had asked the Reverend Samuel Doak to speak to the men. After the early morning worship, the men started their march up Gap Creek with the battle cry, "The Sword of the Lord and Gideon."

SAMUEL DOAK'S FAMOUS SERMON AND PRAYER

AT SYCAMORE SHOALS MUSTER SEPTEMBER 1780

"My countrymen, you are about to set out on an expedition which is full of hardships and dangers, but one in which the Almighty will attend you.

"The Mother Country has her hands upon you, these American Colonies, and takes that for which our fathers planted their homes in the wilderness—OUR LIBERTY.

"Taxation without representation and the quartering of soldiers in the homes of our people without their consent are evidence that the Crown of England would take from its American Subjects the last vestige of Freedom.

"Your brethren across the mountains are crying like Macedonia unto your help. God forbid that you shall refuse to hear and answer their call—but the call of your brethren is not all. The enemy is marching hither to destroy your homes.

"Brave men, you are not unacquainted with battle. Your hands have already been taught to war and your fingers to fight. You have wrested these beautiful valleys of the Holston and Watauga from the savage hand. Will you tarry now until the other enemy carries fire and sword to your very doors? No, it shall not be. Go forth then in the strength of your manhood to the aid of your brethren, the defense of your liberty and the protection of your homes. And may the God of Justice be with you and give you victory."

"Let Us Pray"

"Almighty and gracious God! Thou hast been the refuge and strength of Thy people in all ages. In time of sorest need we have learned to come to Thee—our Rock and our Fortress. Thou knowest the dangers and snares that surround us on march and in battle.

"Thou knowest the dangers that constantly threaten the humble, but well beloved homes, which Thy servants have left behind them.

"O, in Thine infinite mercy, save us from the cruel hand of the savage, and of tyrant. Save the unprotected homes while fathers and husbands and sons are far away fighting for freedom and helping the oppressed.

"Thou, who promised to protect the sparrow in its flight, keep ceaseless watch, by day and by night, over our loved ones. The helpless woman and little children, we commit to Thy care. Thou wilt not leave them or forsake them in times of loneliness and anxiety and terror.

"O, God of Battle, arise in Thy might. Avenge the slaughter of Thy people. Confound those who plot for our destruction. Crown this mighty effort with victory, and smite those who exalt themselves against liberty and justice and truth.

"Help us as good soldiers to wield the SWORD OF THE LORD AND GIDEON."

"AMEN"

The sermon and prayer of Samuel Doak are used through the courtesy of Mrs. Rollo H. Henley, Washington College, Tennessee. It is taken from the scrapbook of her father, J. Fain Anderson.

Sycamore Shoals Muster, where the Overmountain Men assembled before leaving for the King's Mountain Campaign. The date was September 25, 1780. So anxious were the men and boys to go they had to draft those who were needed to remain and protect the home front. Women and children, boys and girls came to see their husbands, fathers, and loved ones off on this hazardous undertaking. Colonel John Sevier had asked his friend Samuel Doak to conduct services for the men. This picture is a reproduction of a painting by Lloyd Branson. The original hangs in the State Capitol, Nashville. It is used by courtesy of the Tennessee Department of Conservation.

22

THE TRAIL TOWARDS FERGUSON

Shelving Rock

The first night's camp was at Shelving Rock (sometimes called Resting Place) near the present town of Roan Mountain. Under the shelter of this rock, powder, meal and other supplies were stored. Many of the pioneers had their horses shod by John Miller, a blacksmith of that vicinity. A council, held under the rock, made plans for crossing the mountains and a faster march. The herd of cattle was slowing the progress of the men; so it was decided to slaughter and cook sufficient meat

Bright's Settlement

Bright's Branch

for the mountain crossing. The remainder of the herd was driven back to the settlements. Much time was consumed the morning of the 27th with this chore, but it saved time in the long run.

They reached the Bald of Roan Mountain in the afternoon. Here the men ate lunch and drilled in snow, ankle deep. Militia drilling was a new experience for these pioneer Indian fighters. Rolls were called by companies. It was discovered that two men of Sevier's company, with Tory leaning, were not present. The commanding officers decided to change their route. The British might be nearer than they had thought. They turned down Elk's Hollow, following Bright's Trace. This was a trail used by Bright traveling to and from his hunting camp. They camped the second night, September 27th, near the mouth of Bright's Branch where it flowed into Roaring Creek.

Bright's Trace

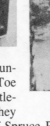
Grassy Creek

On the morning of September 28th, they followed the Yellow Mountain Trail (Bright's Trace) as it meandered along Roaring Creek to Toe River. They followed this trail along Toe River through Bright's Settlement, to Cathee's Place near the mouth of Grassy Creek, where they camped the third night. This campsite is near the present town of Spruce Pine, North Carolina.

The next day they traveled up the valley of Grassy Creek to Gillespie's Gap on the Blue Ridge. Here it was decided to divide the force in case the British should try to ambush their troops. Colonel Campbell led his men down through the Turkey Cove route, and they camped near Colonel Wofford's Fort. During the night an attempt was made to get information from Henry Gillespie, a Tory living in Turkey Cove.

Gillespie was so far removed from any contact with the war, that he had no useful information. Gillespie and Wofford had taken the oath, under Ferguson, more of necessity that from any sense of allegiance. Gillespie's descendants had a pass issued by Ferguson. They were so ashamed of this paper they kept it hidden for years.

Sevier and Shelby led their men down through the North Cove of Catawba Creek, and camped near Honeycutt's Creek. It was here that Colonel Charles McDowell met with these two commanders who had started the campaign. McDowell reported that scouts placed Ferguson at Gilbert Town, and that Colonel Cleveland and Major Winston were approaching with a force of three hundred fifty men. Charles McDowell, who had left Watauga several days before the Overmountain men, had sent James Blair to inform Cleveland and Winston of the mountaineers' movements. Blair had been wounded by a Tory while on this mission, but was able to reach Cleveland at Fort Defiance. McDowell had also gained the information that Sumpter's men, under the command of Generals Hill, Lacey, and Hawthorne, were close enough to join in the march against Ferguson.

Legend has stated that the Seviers spent the night of September 29th in this cabin. A post office and a school nearby were named Sevier.

On September 30th, the two forces were reunited, and continued on to the Catawba River and along its banks, crossing the Linville River, finally arriving at Quaker Meadows (Morganton, North Carolina). Here at the McDowell home, they were given fresh meat from the hidden beefs driven from the mountain gorges. The McDowell brothers insisted on the use of dry fence rails to build their fires. Many of McDowell's men who had remained behind rejoined the force. During the night Colonel Benjamin Cleveland with the men from Wilkes County, and Major Joseph Winston and his company from Surry County, joined the Overmountain men, bringing the total force to about fourteen hundred.

Joseph Winston

24

The ridge in right center separates two creeks. Cane River flows on view side of ridge. Silver Creek flows on the beyond side.

On Sunday morning October 1st, the march was resumed. A good road made for faster progress. During the afternoon, a heavy rain set in. They made camp early in South Mountain Gap, near the head of Cane and Silver Creeks. Pilot Mountain, well-known landmark, could be seen from campsite. Another name for the place is Bedford's Hill. This was near the battle site where McDowell's force was attacked by a force of Ferguson's men a few weeks earlier.

The next day it continued to be wet and rainy, so the army remained in camp. The unaccustomed discipline and restraint caused unrest and occasional fights among the men. This gave the officers much concern. It was generally agreed that a definite military organization must be set up and campaign plans made.

The officers met during the evening of October 2nd for a conference. Colonel Charles McDowell, being the senior officer present, presided. It was brought out that there should be a military head for the entire force. The coming of various companies from several sections resulted in the fact that no one was properly in command of the whole. It was decided that a messenger be sent to headquarters at Hillsborough, North Carolina, to ask General Gates to send a commanding officer to take charge of the entire army.

This proposed delay greatly irked Colonel Shelby, Sevier and their associate officers from across the mountains. It was then proposed that the officers meet daily for consultation, and that one of their number be chosen as officer of the day. This officer was to carry out plans formulated at the staff meeting the preceding day. This plan still did not satisfy Shelby. With Ferguson reported so near, Shelby argued that the combined forces needed a firm leader of known experience—a leader that would pursue the objective with all promptness. All the commanding officers were North Carolinians, save Colonel William Campbell, who was from Virginia. Shelby said he knew Colonel Campbell to be a man of good sense, and sincerely devoted to the cause of his country. Also, Colonel Campbell commanded the largest regiment. Shelby thus proposed Campbell's name for consideration. Shelby closed with the proposal that Colonel Campbell be made the commanding officer, until the designated officer should arrive from headquarters, and that they march at once against the enemy.

It is said that Campbell took Shelby aside and requested his name be withdrawn. Campbell asked Shelby that he, himself, consent to serve in the capacity of commanding officer. Shelby replied that he was the youngest Colonel present, and that he had served under Colonel McDowell, a fine man but slow of action for such an enterprise as this.

Cane Creek   Pilot Mountain

Shelby feared that Colonel McDowell might take offense should he, Shelby, be placed in command over him. Campbell agreed to this reasoning. In the meeting of the staff, this proposal was agreed upon and adopted. Colonel Shelby states that he made the proposal to silence the expectations of Colonel Charles McDowell — a brave, patriotic and good man, but too inactive for such a command. He lacked the tact and efficiency called for in handling a campaign of this magnitude. Colonel McDowell had the tendency to send rather than to lead. Some of the officers expressed the desire that either General William Lee Davidson or General Daniel Morgan be sent to take command of the force. (A conference, concerning the selection of a commanding officer, was held by the Overmountain officers on top of Roan Mountain during their stop there.)

GENERAL DANIEL MORGAN

General Daniel Morgan was one of the finest of Revolutionary War officers. He was largely responsible for victories at Stillwell and Saratoga. Gates never mentioned him in his report to congress. His last and outstanding victory was at Cowpens, South Carolina, January 17, 1781. Bad health caused his retirement shortly afterwards. Morganton, North Carolina, was named in his honor.

General William Lee Davidson, from Charlotte, North Carolina, was beloved by all Carolinians and Tennesseans. He was a gallant officer and gentleman. He was assisting Morgan escape with prisoners when killed February 1st, 1781. Davidson County, Tennessee, was named in his honor.

GENERAL WILLIAM LEE DAVIDSON

Colonel Charles McDowell, who had the good of the country at heart more than the title to command, submitted gracefully to the decision. McDowell also suggested that, if agreeable, they let him convey to general headquarters the request for a commanding officer. This was warmly approved. A sincere ovation was given McDowell, who was warmed by the grand manner in which this proposition was presented to his fellow officers. He turned his command over to his brother, Major Joseph McDowell. Thus Colonel William Campbell became temporary commander of the army that was on the warpath against Colonel Patrick Ferguson and his Tory Force.

Major Joseph McDowell, commanding Patriots from Burke County, North Carolina

THE "GAMECOCK"

Colonel Thomas Sumpter, nicknamed the "Gamecock", used the title of Colonel but held no commission. The men in his force, at the time of the King's Mountain Battle, were mostly exiles from Loyalist persecution in South Carolina. They just sort of banded together and selected Sumpter as their leader. Many of their homes, including Sumpter's, had been burned and their families were refugees. These men were not receiving any government pay or backing. They were only interested in fighting the British with any responsible group. They furnished their own horses, guns, and equipment. Some would just tag along until they could get a horse and gun from a fallen comrade or a slain enemy.

Abner Nash, Governor of North Carolina

Governor Abner Nash of North Carolina, through the influence of Governor Rutledge, had given Colonel Williams permission to recruit in North Carolina. Williams made his headquarters in Rowan County. Governor Nash had also promised supplies from the limited commissaries of the state. Colonel Williams promised beef, bread and potatoes, in his call to arms. New recruits, and the addition of a company of South Carolinians under Colonel Thomas Brandon and Major Samuel Hammond, brought Williams' command to the approximate number of seventy; and learning the location of Sumpter's men, Williams moved in that direction. He had been repulsed by Sumpter and his men in an earlier attempt to take over the command. He decided to try again.

Colonel Sumpter, and many of his regular officers, had gone to Hillsborough to confer with Governor Rutledge, regarding Williams' attempt to take over his command. Colonel William Hill was left in charge during this period. Meanwhile, the troops were marching to form a junction with General William Lee Davidson, then in charge of the Salisbury District Militia.

The Sumpter Force, under Hill's command, arrived at the foot of Flint Mountain (presently known as Cherry Mountain) October 3rd. On this same day, Colonel Charles McDowell, enroute to general headquarters, visited these men. McDowell explained the purpose and extent of the mountaineer campaign, and invited the South Carolinians to join in the march against Ferguson. During the same day, Colonels William Graham and Frederick Hambright, and some fifty or sixty men from Lincoln County, North Carolina, joined the Sumpter group. Colonel James Williams again visited the camp and demanded the post of commanding officer. Again he was refused. So strong was the feeling against Williams, that he moved his camp some distance away. Colonel Hill, suffering from a wounded arm received in a recent battle, placed Colonel Edward Lacey in active charge of the force.

In a council, it was decided that Colonel Lacey visit the camp of the Overmountain men, and find out more

about their plans. Also, scouts with recent information regarding Ferguson's location had arrived in camp. Lacey set out, the night of October 5th, and traveled toward Gilbert Town. The night trip was a hard one, but he finally found the camp at Alexander's Ford on Green River.

Flint Mountain, later called Cherry Mountain

The Patriot Army assembled at Bedford Hill before the march to Gilbert Town

The mountaineer army, thinking Ferguson some fifteen miles away at Gilbert Town, made preparation for the conflict. Before breaking camp, Colonel John Sevier assembled the troops for a meeting. Colonels Cleveland, Campbell, Shelby, Sevier, McDowell, Winston and other officers entered the circle of men. With eloquent words of wisdom, the two-hundred-fifty-pound jovial Cleveland spoke first. He told them of the priceless opportunity of service to their country, and a rich heritage to their children. Cleveland also offered the weak-hearted a chance to back out. After a moment for consideration, Major Joseph McDowell, with his personable smile, asked, ''what kind of story would they relate when they arrived back home, while their comrades were fighting for their country?''

Shelby then proposed that those who desired to leave step three paces to the rear. Not a man accepted this invitation. A murmur of applause rose from the men, who seemed proud of each other. Quote from Shelby: ''I am heartily glad to see you, as a man, resolved to meet and fight your country's foes. When we encounter them, don't wait for the word of command. Let each of you be your own officer and do the best you can, taking every care of yourselves, and availing yourselves of every advantage that chance may throw your way. If in the woods, shelter yourselves and give them Indian play. Advance from tree to tree pressing the enemy, killing and disabling all you can. Your officers will shrink from no danger. They will be constantly with you, and the moment the enemy gives way, be on the alert and strictly obey orders.''

With this appeal and advice, the troops were dismissed with directions to be ready to march within three hours. Provisions for two meals were to be prepared and placed in their knapsacks. Colonels Cleveland and McDowell had somehow secured whisky, which they added as a treat for the men.

Breaking camp, they marched down Cane Creek a few miles, and stopped for the night near the home of Samuel Andrews, a loyal Whig. Placing guards around the camp, they slept on their arms. The next morning, October 4th, they continued their march. After crossing Cane Creek several times, the mountain men reached the vicinity of Gilbert Town about nightfall. They learned from Jonathan Hampton that Ferguson and his Tories had left that area, and Hampton told them it was rumored that they were headed southward toward Fort Ninety-Six.

Home of Samuel Andrews built in 1740. Both armies camped near this house: Ferguson, after the Battle with McDowell's men; the Overmountain men enroute to King's Mountain. Andrews lost all of his stock and food supplies to the Tories. He had to hide in the hills for safety.

THE MOUNTAIN CROSSING

Colonel Elijah Clarke, encouraged by the success at Musgrove's Mill, took leave of Shelby and McDowell and returned to Georgia. Recruiting more troops as he led his men along a foothill route, he made plans for a series of harassing attacks against the Loyalist forces in his home settlements. Clarke soon learned of the big stock of supplies stored in the depot at Augusta. These supplies were for the proposed Indian campaign against the settlers of the Watauga and Nolichucky districts. Clarke and his men laid siege to Augusta on September 14th, 15th, and 16th, 1780. This attack would have succeeded but for a party of Cherokee and Creek warriors arriving in Augusta for these supplies. Enraged at having their way blocked in getting the guns and ammunition, they attacked from the rear. Clarke, unable to withstand an attack from both sides, had to retreat. This relief gave Cruger the needed time to arrive with reinforcements from Ninety-Six. Colonel Clarke was forced to run. With his force and some four hundred women, children and old folk (families of his men), he fled toward the mountains.

Several patriots had been taken prisoner by the Tories. Captain Ashby and twelve of his men were hung immediately. Thirteen were turned over to the Indians to be tortured and put to death Indian-style. Colonel Browne, wounded several times during the siege, was determined to wreak his vengeance on any American within reach. Over thirty were hung, tomahawked and shot.

A report of this Battle and its outcome was sent to Colonel Ferguson, who immediately sent detachments out in hopes of intercepting Clarke. Captain Alexander Chesney did get near enough to catch one prisoner and return him to Ferguson. One of the British Lieutenants commented, ''There were several whom they immediately hanged and have a great many more yet to hang. We have now a method that will put an end to the rebellion in a short time, by hanging every man that has taken protection and is found acting against us.''

Colonel Clarke, with remnants of his force, and the four hundred women and children headed for the mountains. They were constantly harassed from the rear by bands of Tories and Indians. His faithful followers were able to ward off most of the attacks and allow the main party to gain the safety of the mountains. The Indian and Tory attackers would fall on the old men and women who were unable to keep pace with the main body. Occasionally, young boys would be captured and taken to the Tory camp.

At night the captured boys would be stripped of their clothes and made to dance between two hot fires until burned to death. Old men would be dismembered, scalped and limbs of their bodies hung on tree branches. The atrocities committed were almost too ghastly to relate. These stories were told to the Overmountain men, by Major Candler and his men, when they arrived at Gilbert Town. Captain Edward Hampton, who was scouting in that part of the country, had informed the Clarke people of the Campaign then in progress against Ferguson.

It took Colonel Clarke and his refugees many days to make the mountain crossing of about two hundred miles. The scant food supplies were reserved for the children. The adults lived entirely on nuts, berries and whatever food could be obtained from the forests. The entire party was near starvation when they arrived in the Nolichucky settlements.

Clarke leads his people across the mountains

The generous people of the Nolichucky and Watauga communities opened their hearts and homes to these refugee Georgian Patriots in distress. Colonel Clarke and his family were received into the Sevier home and remained there until conditions were such that they could return to Georgia.

Colonel Patrick Ferguson

THE ELUSIVE FERGUSON

Colonel Ferguson, receiving Cruger's message regarding Colonel Clarke's defeat at Augusta and consequent retreat toward the hills, immediately left Gilbert Town and marched south in hopes of intercepting the Georgians. He made camp at James Step's place near Green River. Detachments were sent out in several directions in an effort to locate Clarke's route of retreat. It was at the Green River camp that James Crawford and Samuel Chambers, the two Tory defectors from the Overmountain force, joined the Ferguson Camp.

This report, of the large back-water army advancing toward him, rudely awakened the British Colonel from his sense of security. He suddenly realized that his threat of hanging, fire, and sword, had aroused a giant to come after him. Having tarried in this sector longer than planned, in trying to capture Clarke, Ferguson knew that he had to move.

Dispatches were prepared asking for reinforcements. One message, written to General Cornwallis, was sent by Abram Collins and Peter Quinn. Delaying tactics were employed by watching Whigs. Two sons of Alexander Henry followed the Tory messengers. Collins and Quinn saw the Henry boys lurking on their trail. Afraid for their lives, they hid by day, and traveled by night. These maneuvers slowed the messengers to such an extent that they did not reach the camp of Cornwallis until October 7, the day of the battle. Colonel Cruger, in his reply to Ferguson, stated that he did not have half the number requested in his garrison. It was at this stage that Ferguson had the rumor spread that he was marching toward Fort Ninety-Six.

The Tory commander's elusive route and whereabouts caused the Overmountain men some delay and confusion. This was part of the British Colonel's strategy, in trying to work himself out of a difficult situation. He wanted to trap Clarke and his Georgians and he needed time to recall his furloughed men. Ferguson was also probably debating in his mind, should he join Cornwallis in Charlotte or fight the hated Indian-yelling mountaineers.

From the diary of Lieutenant Anthony Allaire of Ferguson's Corps, these entries are noted: October 1, "got in motion at five o'clock in the afternoon and marched twelve miles to Dennard's Ford where we lay 8th September." Monday 2nd, "got in motion at four o'clock in the afternoon and forded Broad River; marched four miles; formed in lines of action and lay on our arms. This night I had nothing but the canopy of heaven to cover me." Tuesday 3rd, "got in motion at four o'clock in the morning; marched six miles to Camp's Ford of Second Broad River, forded it and continued on six miles to one Armstrong's plantation, on the banks of Sandy Run. Halted to refresh; at four o'clock got in motion, forded Sandy Run; marched seven miles to Buffalo Creek; forded it; marched a mile further and halted near Tate's plantation." Friday 6th, "got in motion at four o'clock in the morning, marched sixteen miles to little King's Mountain, where we took up our ground."

The two-day halt at Tate's plantation was most likely made to wait for the furloughed men to report, and to get fresh information from scouts as to the whereabouts of the Patriot army. Messages to Cornwallis indicate this line of reasoning. Colonel Ferguson seemed unaware that none of his messengers were getting through to Cornwallis. He underestimated the calibre of this hardy force of Indian fighters that had crossed the mountains just to fight him.

Mountain on which famous battle was fought.

MESSAGE TO CORNWALLIS: "My Lord: - A doubt does not remain with regard to the intelligence I sent your Lordship. They are since joined by Clarke and Sumpter—of course are becoming an object of some consequence. Happily their leaders are obliged to feed their followers with such hopes; and so to flatter them with accounts of our weakness and fear, that if necessary, I should hope for success against them myself; but numbers compared, that must be doubtful."

"I am on my march towards you, by a road leading from Cherokee Ford, north of King's Mountain. Three or four hundred good soldiers, part dragoons, would finish the business. Something must be done. This is their last push in this quarter, etc."

Colonel Ferguson was evidently expecting more of his furloughed men under Colonel John Moore and Major Zachariah Gibbs to report. Not knowing that his messages were not reaching General Cornwallis on schedule, he had false hopes of his reinforcements. Colonel Banistre Tarleton, recovering from a siege of fever, was unable to lead a platoon. Colonel Cruger's militia from Fort Ninety-Six would not arrive in time to help. Colonel Patrick Ferguson, thinking that reinforcements would come, dreamed grandiose visions of defeating the hated backwater men. He thought that King's Mountain afforded him an ideal spot for such an encounter, and that he could withstand any force the rebels could muster against him. He is reputed to have said that, "God Almighty could not drive him from it."

Part of King's Mountain Range

King's Mountain Range took its name from a family of that name who lived at the foot of the range. King's Creek has the same name origin. The entire range, some sixteen miles in length, extends generally from the northeast in North Carolina, to a southwest direction in South Carolina. Spurs jut out in many directions along its course. The principal elevation is a tower called the "Pinacle". This promontory is nearly six miles from the battleground. Crowder Mountain is the tall hill at the northeast end of the range. The mountain on which the battle was fought is in York County, South Carolina. This promontory is approximately six hundred yards long and about two hundred feet from base to base. The rocky summit of the mountain stands some sixty feet above the surrounding terrain. Its ridge surface, along the six hundred yards, varies from sixty to one hundred feet in width. It is narrow enough that a man, standing on it, can be shot from either side.

A spring on the northwest side furnished sufficient water for the men and horses of Ferguson's army. There were trees to build breastworks, but none were built. About the only thing done of a defensive nature, was to place the wagons and baggage along the northeast ridge of the mountain near his headquarters. Here he waited for the return of his furloughed men who never came. Vainly, he looked for the reinforcements from Cornwallis and Cruger. Instead there came those hated Indian-yelling, vagabond backwater men. Ferguson's exaggerated dependence on the bayonet, and infatuation for military glory, is the only plausible explanation for his remaining on King's Mountain.

The King's Mountain Battleground, showing the north slope of the ridge, on the left, and the original Chronicle marker in the background. Sketched by Benson J. Lossing during his visit to the area on January 8, 1849.

THE GHOST LEGION

Mouth of Cane Creek

Now, back to the Overmountain men at Gilbert Town. The Commanding Officers were greatly dismayed at finding their quarry had fled. Jonathan Hampton, a loyal Whig and son of Colonel Andrew Hampton, told the officers that Ferguson had left several days earlier and headed south. During a staff meeting, called to discuss their next move, Major William Candler with thirty Georgians from Clarke's force, marched into camp. They had no news of Ferguson, as they had traveled a back route.

The Americans, more determined than ever, marched in the direction of Ninety-Six. At Probit's Place, near Broad River, Major William Chronicle with twenty men from Lincoln County, North Carolina, joined the growing army. Each addition was hailed with much enthusiasm. The many small companies, weak by themselves, were becoming a formidable force by uniting together.

Following the same general direction and route they thought Ferguson had followed, this legion of rugged fighters crossed Mountain Creek, and then Broad River at Dennard's Ford. Here they lost sight of Ferguson's trail. Scouts were sent out in every direction to search for information. The Patriots continued on to Alexander's Ford on Green River, crossed and made camp on what was later known as Alexander's farm. Many of the horses were limping, and some of the foot-soldiers were footsore and showing signs of strain, in their effort to keep pace with the march. The leaders were worried and concerned about the situation. They realized that Ferguson, with several days' start, could elude them unless they moved faster.

Alexander's Ford on Green River

In a staff meeting it was decided to select the best riflemen and the best horses, in order to speed up the chase. Most of the night of October 5 was spent accomplishing this task. About seven hundred were chosen. A strong guard, changed every two hours, was posted around the camp. Rumors, picked up by the returning scouts, indicated that Ferguson had marched to Fort Ninety-Six. This stronghold, recently repaired and strengthened, was reputed to be impregnable against an attack by small arms. Not deterred, the mountaineers made plans to move in that direction.

During this all-night session at Green River, Colonel Edward Lacey rode into camp. He had some difficulty gaining access to the Command Officers. The suspicious guards thought he might be a Tory spy. This visit by Lacey was most opportune, as it gave direction and focus to the march. Colonel Lacey told of McDowell's visit to their camp and invitation to join the campaign. He was able to give definite news of Ferguson's general location and strength. One of his scouts, pretending to be a Loyalist, had stayed in the Tory Camp for a day or two. Lacey urged the leaders to push on and engage the British before reinforcements could arrive. Delay might prove fatal to their success. This plan was heartily approved.

Before leaving, Lacey promised to lead his force for a junction with the mountaineers at Cowpens the next day, October 6. On arrival at the South Carolinian camp, about ten o'clock in the morning, he related the prospects of the march against Ferguson to his fellow officers. The reaction was for moving immediately, as they broke camp and began the twenty odd miles trek, toward Cowpens. They arrived there shortly after the mountaineers.

The seven hundred horsemen left the Green River Camp early Friday morning. They traveled to Sandy Plains, and from there followed the ridge road in a southeastern direction. Colonel Campbell had placed the foot soldiers under the commands of Major Joseph Herndon, Major Patrick Watson, Captain William Neal, Captain Richard Allen and other necessary officers. He asked them to follow as speedily as possible as they might be greatly needed in a prolonged battle. It has been well established that some fifty footmen reached the scene of the battle just moments after it was finished. Some historians have insisted that some of the foot soldiers were actually in the battle.

Cowpens was so named because a wealthy English Tory ran a big cattle ranch there and had constructed many pens to herd his cattle. Sanders, pulled out of bed and questioned about Ferguson's whereabouts, was unable to give them any information regarding the Tory force. They had not passed that way.

During the Cowpens stop, the Americans slaughtered several cattle from the Sanders herd. Fires dotted the night as the men roasted the meat. A field of corn was harvested in short order for the horses. This rest and food would be the last that men and horses would get for many long, hard, weary hours. During this stop, a crippled scout named Joseph Kerr caught up with the army. Kerr had passed himself off as a Tory and spent some time in the British Camp. Kerr mixed among the men and gained much information without arousing suspicion. He stated that Ferguson planned to camp on Little King's Mountain. His news heartened the Patriot force and quickened their anticipation of overtaking the enemy.

The estimate of the entire American army, according to Draper, is 1,840 including footmen. The number that left Sycamore Shoals was 1,040 plus or minus a few. This included the Virginians under Campbell, the Sullivan County men with Shelby, the Watauga and Nolichucky Indian fighters with Sevier, and the North Carolinians from Burke County with McDowell. At Quaker Meadows the addition of the Surry Countians with Winston and Wilkes County men under Cleveland brought the total to about 1,390; Candler's thirty Georgians and Chronicle's twenty Lincoln Countians brought the total to 1,440. The addition of the South Carolinians, under Hill, Lacey, Hawthorne, Hambright, Graham and Williams brought the entire force to the 1,840 count.

Two hundred of the best riflemen and horses were selected from the South Carolinians. This brought the total horsemen to something like 910. This mounted force left Cowpens about nine o'clock Friday night, October 6. Shelby says, "it was dark, cold, cloudy and rainy, and that at times a heavy downpour." The roads were difficult to follow in the murky blackness. The scouts, leading Campbell's force up front, took the wrong road, and several companies became lost from the main body. It was morning before the missing men had been located and reunited with their regiment. The plan to cross Broad River at Tate's was discarded for the reason that Ferguson might have guards stationed on the eastern bank. Cherokee Ford, some two and one-half miles south, was thought to be safer. As they approached the river, Enoch Gilmer, a scout, was sent to check on possible sentries. They soon heard him singing "Barney Lynn", the all clear signal. It was daylight when they made the cold wet crossing. Eighteen miles had been covered since leaving Cowpens. King's Mountain was still fifteen miles away.

The cold hard night's travel through rain and slush had made many of the men discontented, grumpy and surly; and the rain still fell. Campbell, Sevier and Cleveland felt that a halt, to let men and horses rest, would help matters. They approached Shelby with this suggestion. He replied, "I will not stop until night if I follow Ferguson into Cornwallis' lines." Without a word of reply, the three officers returned to their places and the march continued.

About seven miles from the river crossing, two Tories were captured at Solomon Beason's house. Beason changed his loyalty as the occasion required. With a little persuasion, the two men told the Mountaineers that Ferguson was camped on Little King's Mountain and agreed to pilot them there. Along the way, two other Tories were captured, and their story corroborated this information. For the first time in several days, this Ghost Legion, composed of several different small companies, had a definite foe ahead on King's Mountain.

Keeping a wary eye in all directions, guarding against a surprise ambush, the army moved onward. Rounding a turn in the road, the leaders saw a familiar horse hitched in front of a house. It belonged to Gilmer, who was scouting ahead of the columns of marching men. Campbell and some of the officers entered the house. They found Gilmer, enjoying a homecooked meal served by two attractive ladies. With a big show of capture and much abusive language, they placed a noose around the scout's neck with angry threats of hanging then and there. Major Chronicle begged Campbell and the other officers, in deference to the ladies, that they not hang the man until they had passed beyond sight of the house. With the rope around his neck, Gilmer was led away by the Americans and

Broad River

released when some distance down the road. The scout related how he had passed himself off as a Tory looking for the British camp, in order to sign up. One of the women told him that she had visited the Tory camp that morning, with chickens for the Commander. She described the location of the camp by saying it was on a King's Mountain ridge, between two creeks where a hunter's camp was set up. Chronicle and Mattox spoke up and said they had used this camp on several occasions, when hunting in that section. They were thus able to give a good description of the terrain and approaches.

With this information, concerning the lay of the land and the position of the Tory camp, the officers withdrew and held a council. The plan of action was mapped out and each Commanding Officer assigned a definite sector of the mountain. Each company was supposed to reach their position before the signal for attack was given. As the rain had stopped at noon, and the sun was shining bright, the spirits of the men brightened with the day.

The officers returned to their various commands and explained the plan of battle and the general arrangements of the troops around the mountain. The men were told that by shooting uphill they were less likely to hit their comrades. Also they would be less likely to be hit by the British, who in shooting downhill would overshoot. Major Chronicle, with Colonel Hambright's permission, had been placed over Colonel Graham's men. Graham was called home to a sick wife.

Two more Tories, captured by Sevier's men, corroborated the earlier information. John Ponder, a messenger bearing a dispatch to Cornwallis, was taken prisoner a short distance from the mountain. This letter was one asking for immediate assistance. The Americans also learned from Ponder that Ferguson, a well-dressed man, wore a duster over his uniform. Colonel Hambright, of German descent, is supposed to have said, "Well poys when you see dot man mit a pig shirt over his clothes, you may know who him is. Mark him mit your rifles."

About a mile from the mountain the men were halted. They had been traveling in single file, or small scattered squads with little order or regularity. Now two definite battle lines were formed. Colonel Campbell, leading one line in double column, was turning to the right. Colonel Cleveland, leading another double column, turned to the left. Major Chronicle and Colonel Hambright's men had been given a position toward the northeastern end of the mountain, to join forces with Major Winston and close up that portion of the line. Thus, as the various companies reached their positions, the mountain was surrounded with a cordon of the best marksmen in the world. No messenger or troops could escape through this band of iron.

The last general command given to the various officers had been, "When you reach your position, dismount, tie your horse, roll coats and blankets and tie them to the saddle." Then the last part of the order, "Put fresh prime in your guns, and every man go into battle resolved to fight until he dies."

BLOOD ON THE MOUNTAIN

Colonel Ferguson had posted picket lines along the crest of the mountain to its southwestern extremity. This was the most approachable area for an attack. These are the men who first sounded the alarm when the Whig army was sighted. The Rangers and best trained Loyalists would be placed here for the main attack. These soldiers, skilled in the use of bayonets, were dressed in scarlet coats. Ferguson depended on these men for his main defense. The Tory troops recruited in the area, lacking bayonets, had been equipped with long knives fitted by the blacksmith to slip over the muzzle of their guns. These knives served in place of bayonets. No breastworks had been erected from the available trees around the mountain. No reinforcements had arrived to strengthen the British army. The furloughed men being collected by Gibbs and Moore had not arrived. None of the famous plundering Tory bands were with Ferguson on King's Mountain. Among those absent were Captains David Fanning, Bloody Bill Bates, Bloody Bill Cunningham and Sam Brown.

Colonel Ferguson, a vain man, could not imagine that it was possible for him to be defeated. He had never met the hated mountaineers in combat face to face. He disregarded the warning of Captain De Peyster and other officers who had experienced a battle with these riflemen. With no preparation, a false sense of security and visions of glory, Colonel Ferguson waited.

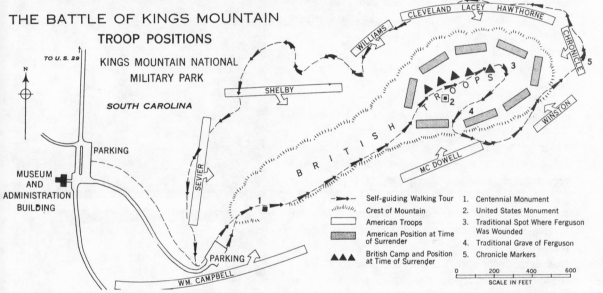

THE BATTLE OF KINGS MOUNTAIN
TROOP POSITIONS
KINGS MOUNTAIN NATIONAL MILITARY PARK
SOUTH CAROLINA

- Self-guiding Walking Tour
- Crest of Mountain
- American Troops
- American Position at Time of Surrender
- British Camp and Position at Time of Surrender

1. Centennial Monument
2. United States Monument
3. Traditional Spot Where Ferguson Was Wounded
4. Traditional Grave of Ferguson
5. Chronicle Markers

SCALE IN FEET

Many conflicting statements are recorded relative to the location of various companies around the battle mountain. The historians of the King's Mountain National Military Park have arranged markers around the mountain in an acceptable manner. With their permission, the author is using their map of location.

Shelby's men had captured a British outpost some distance out, without firing a shot. The main force of mountaineers was within a quarter mile of the Tory position before they were discovered. When the presence of the enemy was reported to Colonel Ferguson, he ordered his men to their positions with beat of drum. The Redcoats fired first on Shelby's men, and he had difficulty in restraining them from advancing. Strict orders had been given not to attack until all commands were in position and the signal given. But the firing from the British had become so regular that Colonel Campbell threw off his coat and yelled at the top of his voice, "Shout like hell and fight like devils." The fierce bloodcurdling Indian yells were taken up by the other companies as they reached their positions and began the attack. Soon the whole mountain was circled with an eerie wail and a burst of gunfire. De Peyster is said to have warned Ferguson of the type of enemy he faced and also remarked, "Those yelling boys are here again."

Cleveland, Chronicle and Winston's men were longer in reaching their positions, as they had a greater distance to travel and the terrain was much rougher. Campbell and Shelby were confronted by the well-trained Rangers, and they bore the brunt of the main attack. This first attack against Campbell and Shelby gave the other officers, who had been delayed, time to reach their positions and open the battle from their sector. As the fight enveloped the mountain, it became volcanic from bottom to top in a sulphuric blaze of thundering guns and smoke.

Colonel Campbell's men were the first to charge up the hill and engage the Rangers. This part of the mountain was steep and rough. The Virginians were met by a fierce charge of fixed bayonets. Many tried to fight it out hand to hand, but guns were no match for sword points, at close range. A fast retreat was made downhill and to the gorge beyond, followed by the Redcoats. Near the foot of the mountain the British Rangers turned and started back to their stations, reloading their guns as they climbed. Ferguson had trained his troops in this style of fighting. By the time the Rangers regained the crest of the incline, Shelby attacked from the other side of the mountain. This gave Colonel Campbell time to reorganize and rally his men for another assault. Campbell's shouted appeal was, "Boys remember your liberty, come on, do it my brave fellows, another gun, another gun will do it." This call, from their leader, seemed to galvanize the Virginians into another spirited attack against the dreaded bayonets.

Almost as Shelby's company retreated, away from the bayonet attack, Campbell and his men would advance up the hill and claim their attention from the other side. This type of charge and counter charge was repeated three times. A description of this part of the fight is given by Captain Chesney, a Tory officer. "By the time the other Americans who had been repulsed had regained their former stations, and sheltered behind trees poured in an irregular and destructive fire. In this manner the engagement was maintained nearly an hour, the mountaineers flying when there was danger of being charged by bayonet, and returning again as soon as the British detachment had faced about to repel another of their parties."

When Shelby's men reached the foot of the hill, he would yell, "Now boys, quickly reload your rifles and let's advance upon them and give them another hell of a fire." Finally Colonel Sevier's Indian fighters had inched their way up rock by rock and tree by tree, until they gained the top and held. By hitting the flank of the enemy, it gave Shelby and Campbell sufficient relief, enabling them to close in from their positions. The men, from all three commands, had become intermingled during the uphill assault. The smoke was so thick and heavy at times, the men could hardly see. But above it all Shelby could be heard, "Shoot like hell and fight like devils."

Meanwhile Colonel Lacey and Hawthorne were making a strong push in their quarter. The South Carolinians had better ground over which to reach their assigned position. They arrived at their post before Cleveland. Colonel Lacey had his horse shot out from under him soon after the battle began. The seasoned troops from York and Chester Counties, South Carolina, gave a good account during the attacks in their sector. No record shows that they were faced with a bayonet charge.

Colonel Cleveland's detachment was about ten minutes late in reaching their position. The swampy ground, flooded by the recent rains, made passage difficult. They were fired upon even before reaching their post. During their march they captured an advance picket with very little trouble. Cleveland, admonishing his men during the battle, could be heard by friend and foe. One of his favorite yells was, "Yonder is your enemy, and the enemy of all mankind." Part of the Wilke's County line was charged by Tories wielding the knife bayonets. During the battle, as his men would advance from tree to tree, Cleveland would shout, "A little nearer to them my brave lads, a little nearer." Roebuck, Cleveland's favorite horse, was killed early in the fight. The Colonel, despite his enormous weight and size, kept up with his front lines on foot. One of his men brought another horse before the conflict was over.

Colonels McDowell and Hampton were holding their positions against an onslaught of bayonets and Tory fire. The loud Indian yells, the constant shrill blast of Ferguson's whistle, two thousand blazing guns, the shouted commands of the officers were all intermingled into a grim nightmare. All this, shrouded with a fog of sulphuric gun smoke, seemed to create a chaotic segment of hell.

Major Chronicle and Colonel Hambright led their Lincoln County troops to the northeastern sector of the mountain. They, like Campbell, had drawn one of the rough and steep slopes of the mountain. As they reached their designated position, Major Chronicle, some steps ahead of his men, shouted, "Face to the hill." Chronicle was killed almost immediately from a volley fired by the Tories above. John Boyd, William Rabb and Captain John Mattox were killed about the same time. The men pressed on to the attack under the leadership of Colonel Hambright, Major Dickson, and Captains White, Espey and Martin. They were charged by a company of Tories using the knife bayonets. As had the other commands, they gave ground, then returned to the fight. Colonel Hambright was wounded toward the close of the battle but continued, even as his boot filled with blood.

The sector of the mountain assigned to Major Winston was more difficult to reach than some of the others. It was a very important position, as his men would form the final link in the encircling chain of riflemen. Major Winston and his Surry County fox hunters had left the main force some distance back, to follow a circuitous route to their position. The terrain was rough and unfamiliar, and they made one or two wrong approaches before finding the right spot. Winston's right wing connected with the left wing of Chronicle, and his left wing with the right wing of McDowell. This closed off the last avenue of escape for either Tory soldier or messenger.

Winston's men escaped a direct charge by the Rangers, as they were posted on the other end of the mountain. The Tory Provincials, stationed in this sector, had little inclination to sally against the sharpshooters lurking below. The many stories about the prowess of these backwoods marksmen gave them caution.

Many stories have been told about Colonel James Williams, some good, some bad. Some say he sulked because his superior rank was not recognized by the General Staff. Others say that he was in the middle of the battle, fighting it out with the bravest. Be that as it may, he gave his life for America. We do have the positive statement saying, in the final charge up the hill, Williams and his men were fighting their way up the slope along with the Sullivan forces under Shelby. Step by step he led his men up the hill against the Rangers. His battle cry was, "Come on boys, the old wagoner never yet backed out." During this fierce charge, the horse Williams was riding was shot out from under him. He continued on foot.

The human slaughter was tremendous. The dead and wounded covered the mountain on the slopes and on the flat. Even before the Mountaineers had gained the crest, Captain De Peyster had urged Ferguson to surrender. He knew the odds were hopeless, and to continue was needless slaughter. Ferguson would have none of it; he still felt that in some way he could win. Surrendering to those hated backwater nothings was impossible. Some of the hardest-fought moments of the battle took place after the Patriots gained the crest of the ridge and were closing in on the Rangers.

Colonel Ferguson, finally realizing that his cause was lost, decided to make a desperate effort to break through the Whig lines. With two companions, he made a sally toward Sevier's position on the hill. Wielding his sword in his left hand, he cut and slashed until his sword was broken. The colonel and two of his fellow officers, Colonel Vessey Husbands and Major Daniel Plummer were shot down by the crack riflemen. These Frontiersmen had come a long way just to get Ferguson. Many have claimed credit for firing the fatal shot. Most historians have credited Robert Young with the deed. Regardless, the bullet that felled Ferguson soon brought the battle to an end.

As the Colonel fell from his horse, his foot caught in the stirrup. The frantic horse dragged the fallen commander around the closing circle of Patriots. It is very likely that many shots were fired into the body during this episode. Each viewing Patriot and Tory could have his own version of what he saw during this dramatic moment. The numerous stories about the shooting of Ferguson had their origin from this incident. We must remember that the battle phobia was at its highest pitch when the Scotchman fell. The stories told and retold would add romantic touches and variations down through the years.

Many conflicting stories are told about where and when the mortal wound of Colonel Williams was sustained. An eyewitness, one of Williams' own men, relates that it was after the white flag of surrender was raised that his Colonel was shot.

Captain Abraham De Peyster, second in command, took charge of the British force after Colonel Ferguson fell. With determined action he continued the fight. De Peyster stubbornly yielded ground, as he gradually pulled his troops back to the cover of the supply wagons where a rally was undertaken. This did not last long, as the encircling Americans soon routed them out of this position. The Tories were finally driven into an area some sixty yards long. De Peyster, realizing the contest was hopeless, raised the white flag of surrender.

Many of the Tories had tied white clothes to their gun sticks and held them up earlier in the battle. Ferguson would cut them down as fast as he saw them hoisted. During the last minutes of the conflict, the scared Loyalists were calling for quarters and mercy. The American password during the campaign was "Buford," and the battle-cry, "Remember Buford and his quarters." They had little compassion or mercy in their hearts. The Tories, sensing this, did not know what to expect from those demon mountaineers. James Sevier

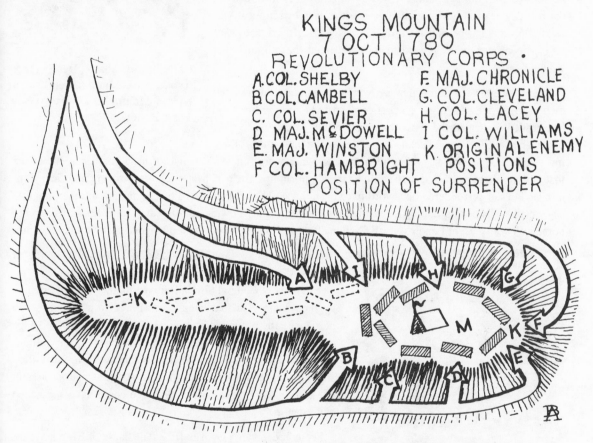

KINGS MOUNTAIN
7 OCT 1780
REVOLUTIONARY CORPS •
A. COL. SHELBY   F. MAJ. CHRONICLE
B. COL. CAMBELL   G. COL. CLEVELAND
C. COL. SEVIER   H. COL. LACEY
D. MAJ. McDOWELL   I. COL. WILLIAMS
E. MAJ. WINSTON   K. ORIGINAL ENEMY
F. COL. HAMBRIGHT   POSITIONS
        POSITION OF SURRENDER

POSITION OF MOUNTAINEER CORPS
ACCORDING TO DRAPER

had heard that his father, Colonel John Sevier, had been killed. This so enraged him that he kept loading his gun and shooting Tories even after the surrender flag had been raised. It was his Uncle Robert that had been mortally wounded.

Some of the Patriot fighters, coming from various sectors of the battle front and not knowing that the British had surrendered, continued to fire as they approached the huddled group. It must be remembered that there was no general communication between the various companies or individuals, as each detachment and frontiersman fought by themselves with little direction. The mountaineers were out to get the renegades that had been causing them so much misery.

With all escape cut off and nowhere to hide from the deadly fire, the Tories thought they would all be killed. Colonel Shelby rode into the middle of this chaotic situation and ordered the Loyalists to lay down their arms, if they expected mercy. Captain Sawyers suggested separating the prisoners from their guns, many of which were found to be loaded. Some firing was still going on when Colonel Campbell arrived at the surrender area. Campbell immediately ordered the Tory officers to group themselves together, sit on the ground and surrender their swords. Before any of these commands could be carried out, a near tragedy occurred. A small party of Tories, returning from a foraging trip, saw the Patriots and began firing. It was more an act of desperation than an attempted attack. Whigs and Tories alike thought that the expected Tarleton and his dreaded Dragoons had arrived. Tories grabbed their guns and began firing on their captors. The Patriots, under Campbell's orders, began firing on the prisoners. It was a very confused aftermath of the battle. Fortunately, the exchange of shots was brief; but it was costly. It was at this point that Colonel James Williams, riding toward the scene of surrender, is said to have received the mortal bullet wound.

Captain Abraham De Peyster, second in command to Ferguson at King's Mountain. Courtesy New York Historical Society.

The prisoners were marched away from their guns and surrounded by a grim cordon of Whigs. The officers, seated on the ground and bareheaded, extended their swords to any Whig officer near. Colonel Campbell, hatless and coatless, passed among their lines collecting swords. One report says that his arms and hands were full. The British officers could hardly believe that this unmilitarily dressed man could be the Commanding Officer. Many reports as to which officer Captain De Peyster surrendered his sword have been made. The broken sword of Ferguson is another enigma. The small whistle used during the battle was taken by Elias Powell, aid-de-camp to Ferguson. Powell's home was near present Lenoir, North Carolina. Colonel Shelby obtained the longer whistle found in camp.

The granite marker at the grave of Major Patrick Ferguson was given by R.E. Scoggins of Charlotte, North Carolina. Stone mound on grave comes from Scottish custom of placing rock cairns on graves.

Historians, have and will, question Ferguson's choice of King's Mountain to make his stand against the mountaineers. One authority, General Simon Bernard, said, "The Americans, by their victory in that engagement, erected a monument to perpetuate the brave men who had fallen there; and the shape of the hill itself would be an eternal monument to the military genius and skill of Colonel Ferguson, in selecting a position so well adapted for defense; and that no other plan of assault but that pursued by the Mountain Men could have succeeded against him."

From Trevelyan's George III, "The battle of King's Mountain has justly been regarded as the turning point in the war in the Southern States. After the catastrophe the Loyalist party was so cowed and prostrate, that military men serving with Lord Cornwallis began to doubt whether such a party any longer existed."

Expert theories and partisan viewpoints come from many quarters as to who did this or did that at King's Mountain. The important thing is, *The Americans Won*. There is a very narrow difference between defeat and victory, or the turn of events that makes one person a hero and the other a villian.

Legend insists that the two women, in the Ferguson camp at King's Mountain, were part of the staff. Both females, said to be very attractive, had most likely been signed on as maids, serving ladies or cooks. Virginia Sal was killed, during the early part of the battle, while helping a wounded soldier to a tent. After the battle was over, many of the curious crowded around to see the fallen Colonel. Tradition says that his clothing was taken from his body for souvenirs, and his naked body was wrapped in a raw beef hide when placed in the grave. Elias Powell, aid-de-camp to Colonel Ferguson, was granted permission to bury his Commander. Another tradition says that, because of the emergency and press of time, Virginia Sal was placed in the same grave. Virginia Paul, of both fact and fiction fame, was taken prisoner as far as Quaker Meadows (Morganton) before being released to return to the Cornwallis Camp.

Ferguson, considered the villian in this episode, conducted himself bravely during the conflict. He did all that mortal man could in trying to prevent total defeat. He was everywhere; his whistle and shout could be heard in all sections of the battleground. He had put too much trust in the bayonet, which was almost useless against the pioneers with their Indian-style warfare. He had two horses shot from under him before his final dash for freedom and death. Many big IF's pop up, as in every conflict. What would have happened if Tarleton had not been sick and made his appearance during the Battle? What would have happened if Cornwallis had received the messages asking for help? What would have happened if the several hundred furloughed men had returned and opened fire from the rear?

The fate of American independence hung in the balance during this fateful hour. This victory changed the course of the war. It greatly subdued the Tories of the two Carolinas. News of the battle fired the Americans with fresh zeal and encouraged the fragments of the scattered Army to reorganize and rise anew. The appearance of this unknown army from out of nowhere that completely annihilated another army, and then disappeared, was something new in military annals. It was a complete surprise to the British. It upset their timetable and turned a successful campaign into one of retreat. It was three days after the battle before Cornwallis fully learned of Ferguson's disastrous and total defeat. He retreated to Winnsboro, South Carolina. Heavy rains and fever-ridden officers (Cornwallis had the fever himself) delayed further activity for some three months. The attitude and cooperation of the Tories completely changed. They feared retaliation from their Whig neighbors for their misdeeds. They refused to join the British forces or support them. The going was harder. All this gave the Patriots renewed hope and time to reorganize. The tide had turned. For this, Clinton blamed Cornwallis, and Cornwallis blamed Ferguson.

The Chronicle Markers: on the left is the original stone, erected 1815, which was replaced with the newer marker in 1914. These stones mark the graves of Major William Chronicle, Captain John Mattocks, William Rabb, and John Boyd; Patriots killed in the battle.

No accurate tabulation of the number of killed and wounded Americans is available. Several men were detailed for this mission but their count did not agree. This Army, made up of many small companies who kept their own rolls, did not have an official roster to check against. Many of these company rolls have been lost or misplaced. Colonels Campbell, Shelby, and Cleveland, in their signed report for General Headquarters, listed twenty-eight killed and sixty wounded. Statements on pension applications would contradict this total, and some of them could be in error.

Regarding the number in the British Army at King's Mountain, the best available estimates place the number near eleven hundred. The American report says: the daily returns for rations was eleven hundred eighty seven (1187); more than one hundred fifty killed; a like number wounded; eight hundred ten prisoners taken. Each writer, in discussing the totals, finds a different answer. The Tory army seems to have been some larger by count than the American force, but the difference is insignificant.

Fifteen hundred stands of arms and a supply of ammunition were found. The seventeen Tory wagons and other supplies that could not be taken by foot or horseback were burned over the campfires that night. The tent cloth was used in making tandem litters to carry the wounded. Very little food supply was found in the Ferguson camp. One keg of rum taken was used in treating the wounded.

It was good dark before the Americans had finished securing their prisoners. The task of caring for the wounded was an all night job. The most severe cases were placed in tents. Dr. Uzal Johnson, the only surviving doctor, attended Tory and Whig alike. Many of the Patriots with minor wounds doctored themselves, as they were accustomed to doing, with herbs and roots.

The Patriots took turns guarding the prisoners during the long, eerie, uneasy night. The best that can be said, it was a night of horror. The dead were scattered over the hill. The moans and groans of the wounded and dying, crying for help and water, mingled with the fear of an expected attack by Tarleton and his Dragoons, made it a soul-searing experience.

Diorama of Battle can be seen at King's Mountain Military Park

42

From Bancroft's *History of the United States:* "The appearance of a numerous enemy from the settlements beyond the mountains, whose names had been unknown to the British, took Cornwallis by surprise; and their success was fatal to his intended expedition. He had hoped to step with ease from one Carolina to another, and from those to the conquest of Virginia; and now he had no choice but to retreat."

From Roosevelt's, *Winning of the West*: "The victory was of far-reaching importance, and ranks among the decisive battles of the Revolution. It was the first great success of the Americans in the South, and the turning point in the Southern Campaign, and it brought cheer to patriots throughout the Union."

An early artist's illustration of the King's Mountain Battle. This print from Draper's "King's Mountain and its Heroes."

"The Battle of King's Mountain."   From a painting by F.C. Yohn.

THE TRAIL BACK

Sunday morning, October 8, about ten o'clock, most of the American force left the mountain battlefield. The fear that Cornwallis would send Tarleton and his Dragoons against them, hurried their departure. The early morning hours were used in constructing tandem horse litters to carry the severely wounded. Nicholas Starnes was placed in charge of the wounded detail during the homeward march. Colonel Campbell dis-

Tandem Horse Litter by Edith Price

patched William Snodgrass and Edward Smith to meet the footsoldiers and direct them to a junction with the main force.

The prisoners were directed to carry one or more of the captured guns, minus flint, with physical ability the determining factor in the number of guns carried. Colonel Shelby stood by to see that this order was obeyed. It was necessary to use the flat of his sword on some objectors.

Colonel Campbell and a company of his men remained behind to bury the dead. A similar detachment of Tories was detained to perform a like duty for their fallen comrades. Several long pits were dug and the slain placed in them side by side. Dr. Uzal Johnson, a British surgeon, had stayed behind to give what aid he could to the wounded. After the battle, Dr. Johnson had treated both Whig and Tory wounded. Many people, both friend and foe, had come to the mountain to find out if a husband, son, brother or neighbor had been killed or wounded. Numerous stories and rumors have been handed down from generation to generation regarding the aftermath of the conflict. Fact and fiction have intermingled to such an extent that the two are hard to separate. Needless to say that any carnage, such as happened on King's Mountain, is bound to leave a pitiful past.

The march away from King's Mountain was necessarily slow. Encumbered with seven or eight hundred prisoners, and wounded comrades, the progress of the tired fighters was greatly slowed. Camp was made the night of October 8, near Broad River between Buffalo and Bowen Creeks, twelve miles from the scene of battle. Colonel James Williams died about three miles from the start of the morning march. The footsoldiers met the returning men and helped set up camp. They had obtained some beeves and located a field of sweet potatoes, which gave the men their first good meal since Friday night at Cowpens. Colonel Campbell,

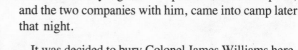

and the two companies with him, came into camp later that night.

It was decided to bury Colonel James Williams here, as it would be almost impossible to take the body home. With full military honors, he was placed in a grave near the mouth of Buffalo Creek.

The grave of Colonel James Williams was later located and the remains moved to a site in the front yard of Gaffney Carnegie Library, Gaffney, South Carolina.

The burial and care of the wounded took up a big portion of the day, but for safety's sake camp was moved some three miles to the north side of Bowen Creek. The leaders hoped to get an early start from here the next morning.

Tuesday morning, October 10, the forces were on the move by good light. They traveled up Broad River, crossing First Broad, Sandy Run, and many other streams as they continued in a northwest direction toward Gilbert Town. They followed the most travelable route leading toward the mountains. Some twenty miles were covered on this march.

The King of England gave land for Brittain Church, built in 1768.

The large body of walking prisoners, strung out in a long thin line, was difficult to guard. Many managed to escape into the forest along the way. Camp was made October 10 near Second Broad River.

Wednesday, October 11, about twelve miles were covered. Camp was made near Gilbert Town on the plantation of Colonel John Walker. A patch of pumpkin, found nearby, was the source of food on this stop. This camp was located about a mile from Brittain Church. The prisoners were placed in bull pens built by Ferguson for Whig prisoners. The Tories were easier to handle here and this respite gave the officers opportunity to handle other complex problems. It was while camped here that the Tory clothing, captured at King's Mountain, was given to the men. One change each was alloted the Tory officers.

Sevier, Shelby and Campbell were faced with a difficult and almost impossible problem in the transportation of their wounded across the mountains. Patriots of that area came to their rescue by offering their homes as havens, until the men were recovered sufficiently to make the trip. Rest and medical care would be available. The records say that Dr. Dobson attended some eighteen of the wounded quartered in Burke County. Most of the day Thursday, October 12, and part of Friday was spent attending this chore. Many individual stories of heroism could be related concerning this chapter of the campaign.

Colonel Campbell and his staff were having other problems that gave them great concern. The Rebels were not treating the captured Tories with the greatest respect. One Tory, taking advantage of an opportunity, threw down his gun and escaped into the woods. Some of his captors found him hiding in a hollow tree. He was dragged out and literally cut to pieces by one of the officers with his captured sword. Many such incidents were happening, causing Campbell to issue a strong order: "I must request officers of all ranks in the army to restrain from the disorderly manner of slaughtering and disturbing the prisoners. If it cannot be stopped by moderate measures, such effectual punishment shall be executed upon delinquents as will put a stop to it."

Another order was directed toward deserting and plundering. Some of the men, hungry, tired, or just plain ornery, were plundering Whig and Tory homes alike. They felt that, having risked their lives in the recent battle, food was due them. Colonel Campbell ordered that "no troops be discharged or released until the prisoners had been delivered to the proper authorities or definite plans for disposal worked out and agreed on by the staff."

Friday, October 13, the army moved to Bickerstaff, sometimes called Red Chimneys. Today the community is called Sunshine. It was here that certain officers of the Carolinas presented complaints to Colonel Campbell. It was stated that among the prisoners were a number of Tories who were robbers, houseburners, parole breakers and assassins. It was also stated that General Cornwallis was responsible for this in his edict, "to subdue the Patriots of South Carolina and Georgia with a cruel hand if necessary." The Southerners who would not take the oath of allegiance were to be treated like criminals.

Whigs who escaped were to be hunted until captured, and their homes burned. In many cases, the women were raped. If a son refused to tell the whereabouts of his father, he was hung. If a wife refused to reveal the location of her husband, her stomach would be ripped open by knife. Tarleton and many of the Tory bandit leaders would force the Tory Americans, under their command, to perform these atrocities. Children, women and old folk were scattered over the countryside, their homes plundered and burned. Many such refugees were found in the woods huddled over a campfire, no food except what they could obtain from the forest. It was felt that if these men were allowed to escape or be paroled, they would continue these deeds. One man told of seeing eleven men hung at Fort Ninety-Six, their only offense being "Whig Rebels."

Bickerstaff Farm where the nine Tories were hung.

Colonel Campbell, on the strength of these complaints, consented to hold court with a copy of North Carolina laws in hand, which stated, "it was legal for two magistrates to summon a jury and hold trial." The law also provided capital punishment. On this basis court was held. A court-martial was ordered. The jury was made up of field Officers and Captains, thus giving the proceedings the status of an orderly court. Witnesses were summoned and examined. The result: thirty-six Tories were convicted and condemned. Right or wrong, the court was legal and handled in proper form.

Some of the Tories brought to trial were released through intercession of neighbors or acquaintances. Among the prisoners were James Crawford and Samuel Chambers. These two men, deserters from Sevier's Corps at Roan Mountain, were released by request of Colonel Sevier. They were told to keep to the straight and narrow and sin no more.

Many of the Patriot officers felt that strong measures were needed to curb the Tory atrocities. This was especially so in the Georgia and South Carolina sections. An eye for an eye was their attitude. If this determined group would set an example, it might halt some of the lawlessness being practiced by the renegades. The officers insisted that they would accept full responsibility for this court action and the executions that might follow. The trials lasted all day and thirty-six were condemned to be hung that night.

A suitable oak tree was selected. For many years this tree was known as "The Gallows Tree." Lines, three and four deep, were formed around the tree, as hand torches lighted the scene. Nine had been hung, three at a time, and the next three made ready when a very unexpected event occurred. Isaac Baldwin was the name of one of the men in the next group to be strung up. He was the leader of a Burke County group of renegade Tories. His reputation of plundering, pillaging and harassing Whigs in that area was well known. As he was waiting for the rope to be placed around his neck, a small lad asked permission to say a farewell to his departing brother. With much crying, wailing and screaming, he made a big show of caressing his brother, as his arms clung in embrace around Isaac's waist. His big show of sorrow and tears completely fascinated the circled soldiers. So intense was their attention, they failed to notice that the young brother, while embracing Isaac, had managed to cut loose the ropes that bound the prisoner's arms behind him. Isaac, free of his bonds, darted through the broken lines of the men and escaped in the darkness. This escape was made through the lines of the best marksmen in the country. They so admired this act of bravery, no effort was made to catch Baldwin. Isaac was killed, shortly after this event, at Bickerstaff's in a fight with a Whig party.

Another man was put in Baldwin's place, and the executioners made ready to continue. Shelby, Sevier and some of the other officers, having a stomach full, put a stop to the hanging. One of the reprieved men told Sevier that he had just received word that Colonel Tarleton, with a strong force, had been sent in pursuit. This was partially true, and easily believed, as such a move had been expected. General Cornwallis, who had received a garbled message of Ferguson's predicament Tuesday, October 10, did send Tarleton to his aid. Tarleton reached a point, near King's Mountain, where full news of the disaster reached him. About the same time a message from Cornwallis, who had also learned the bad news, recalled Tarleton to rejoin his forces retreating toward South Carolina. Thus Tarleton never did give chase to the Ghost Legion.

One of the ironic chapters of this campaign was the two retreating forces, each thinking the other was advancing to attack them. Cornwallis, having heard an exaggerated report of the number of Whig troops, thought that thousands of barbarian mountaineers would be on the march against him. He had practically been unaware of the settlements across the mountains.

Preparations were made for an early march Sunday morning, October 15th. Unencumbered with the wounded, the mountaineer army moved with greater

Catawba River

speed in spite of the rain. The prisoners were prodded with threats and bayonet points to speed the march. The continuous rain made walking tough over muddy roads. The grumbles from the men, both Whig and Tory, were loud and constant, but the leaders would not stop. If the rain continued, which it did, they might get caught this side of the Catawba River. Unable to cross, they would be sitting ducks for Tarleton and his men. On and on they marched, over the muddy road, without food or rest. They reached the river late at night and crossed at Island Ford in waist-deep water. Thirty-two miles had been covered during the day's march. Camp was made on the west bank of the Catawba River on the McDowell farm. These gracious men gave willingly of their seasoned fence rails for fire; more hidden beeves had been brought in to furnish meat; and from somewhere corn meal was provided for bread. For the first time in many

Robertson Creek at Bickerstaff Farm where the Patriots found water for man and beast.

days, with fire to warm and dry their bodies, and food to eat, the men felt safe and relaxed. It was almost a victory celebration, with fires dotting the countryside and a rain-swollen stream between them and Tarleton.

Some of the Tory officers were quartered in the McDowell home. It was just weeks ago that some of these same men had ransacked the house and told Mrs. McDowell, mother of Charles and Joseph, that a rebel's death awaited her sons. It took some persuasion on the part of Joseph to gain Mrs. McDowell's consent for the Tory officers to stay in the house.

During the day, Monday, October 16, the General Staff made plans for dismissing the various companies and disposing of the prisoners. Feeling safe, dry, warm and with a little food in their stomachs, the Patriots were in fine mettle.

Back at Bickerstaff's farm a grim scene, of a different nature, was taking place. As day dawned, the nine dangling bodies could be seen. Mrs. Martha Bickerstaff, with the aid of an old man who helped on the farm, cut the bodies down. Some of the neighbors came and helped dig a trench two feet deep where Colonel Ambrose Mills, Captain Grimes, Captain Walter Gilkey, Captain Wilson, Lieutenant Lafferty, John McFall, John Bebby, and Augustine Hobbs were buried. Friends of Captain Chitwood took his body on a plank to a graveyard at Benjamin Bickerstaff's for burial. Captain Aaron Bickerstaff, husband of Martha, was mortally wounded at King's Mountain. He commanded a Tory Company.

By mutual arrangement, various companies began leaving for their own settlements. Their mission for the moment had been accomplished. Colonels Lacey, Hill, Hawthorn, and the Sumpter forces left for South Carolina. Colonel John Sevier, his men, part of Shelby's force, and the footsoldiers of Colonel Campbell departed for the mountain crossing in the early afternoon of Monday, October 16. With Sevier were the Georgians, under Candler and Johnston, whose families had crossed the mountains with Colonel Clarke. Some of Sevier's and Shelby's men had chosen to remain in the services of McDowell and Cleveland as plans were made for other campaigns.

The mounted men of Campbell's company, troops of Cleveland, Winston and some of McDowell's, formed an escort for the prisoners. They traveled toward the head of the Yadkin River and followed down the valley of that stream toward the headquarters of General Gates.

On their arrival at Bethabara, a Moravian town, Colonels Campbell, Shelby, and Cleveland wrote out their official report and signed it. Here Colonel Campbell issued his final order of the campaign. He appointed Colonel Benjamin Cleveland as Commander of the troops and Official Escort of the prisoners. It was here that Campbell and Shelby took their leave and turned toward home.

Many contributing reasons were responsible for the dwindling number of prisoners. Lieutenant Allaire says that approximately one hundred escaped during one day's march. From all obtainable estimates, only three hundred reached Salem. When the prisoners were delivered to General Gates, it is said, there were less than two hundred.

So, like the Ghost Legion that it was, the victorious army that defeated Ferguson at King's Mountain on October 7, 1780, faded into the mountain fastness and partisan sections from whence it came.

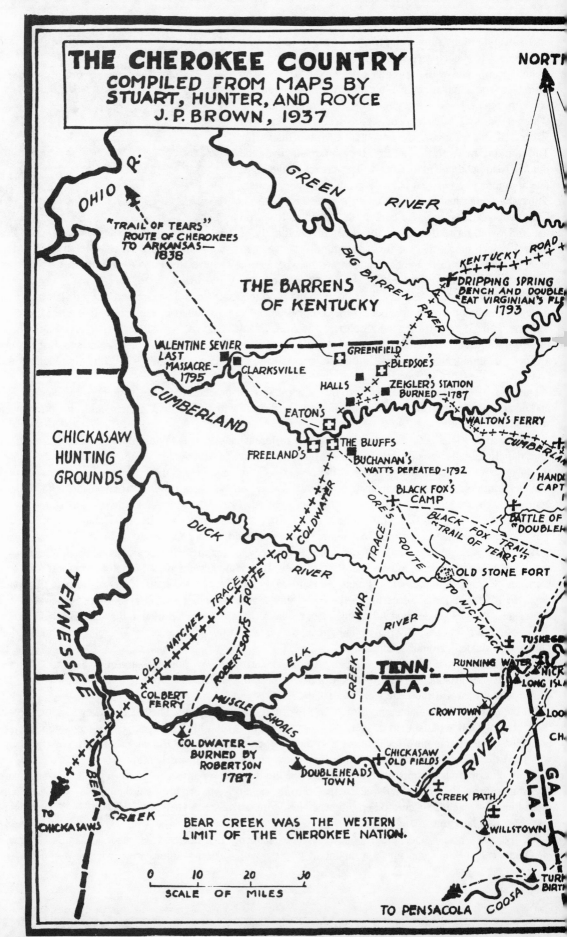

THE CHEROKEE COUNTRY

COMPILED FROM MAPS BY
STUART, HUNTER, AND ROYCE
J. P. BROWN, 1937

NORTH

OHIO R.

GREEN RIVER

BIG BARREN RIVER

"TRAIL OF TEARS"
ROUTE OF CHEROKEES
TO ARKANSAS—
1838

THE BARRENS
OF KENTUCKY

KENTUCKY ROAD

DRIPPING SPRING
BENCH AND DOUBLE
EAT VIRGINIAN'S PLE
1793

VALENTINE SEVIER
LAST
MASSACRE—
1795

CLARKSVILLE

GREENFIELD

BLEDSOE'S

HALLS

ZEIGLER'S STATION
BURNED—1787

CUMBERLAND

EATON'S

WALTON'S FERRY

CUMBERLAND

CHICKASAW
HUNTING
GROUNDS

FREELAND'S

THE BLUFFS

BUCHANAN'S
WATTS DEFEATED—1792

HAND
CAPT

BLACK FOX'S
CAMP

BATTLE OF
"DOUBLEH

DUCK

COLDWATER

ORE'S

BLACK
FOX TRAIL
"TRAIL OF TEARS"

RIVER

WAR TRACE

ROUTE

OLD STONE FORT

TO NICKAJACK

OLD NATCHEZ TRACE

ROBERTSON'S ROUTE TO

ELK

CREEK

RIVER

RIVER

TUSKEG

TENNESSEE

TENN.
ALA.

RUNNING WATER

NICK
LONG ISLA

COLBERT
FERRY

MUSCLE

SHOALS

CROWTOWN

LOO

CH

COLDWATER—
BURNED BY
ROBERTSON
1787

DOUBLEHEAD'S
TOWN

CHICKASAW
OLD FIELDS

RIVER

GA.
ALA.

TO
CHICKASAWS

BEAR CREEK

BEAR CREEK WAS THE WESTERN
LIMIT OF THE CHEROKEE NATION.

CREEK PATH

WILLSTOWN

TURN
BIRTH

0   10   20   30
SCALE OF MILES

TO PENSACOLA

COOSA

48

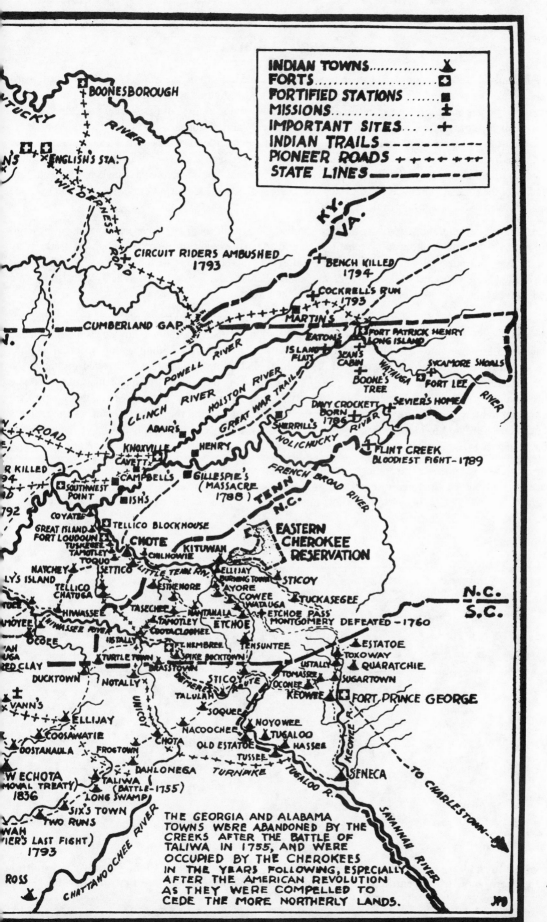

Legend:

INDIAN TOWNS............
FORTS..........................
FORTIFIED STATIONS ......
MISSIONS....................
IMPORTANT SITES.... ...+
INDIAN TRAILS -----------
PIONEER ROADS +++++
STATE LINES

BOONESBOROUGH

KENTUCKY RIVER

ENGLISH'S STA.

WILDERNESS ROAD

KY.
VA.

CIRCUIT RIDERS AMBUSHED
1793

BENCH KILLED
1794

COCKRELLS RUN
1793

CUMBERLAND GAP

MARTIN'S

EATON'S

FORT PATRICK HENRY
LONG ISLAND

ISLAND FLATS

JEAN'S CABIN

WATAUGA

SYCAMORE SHOALS

FORT LEE

BOONE'S TREE

SEVIER'S HOME

POWELL RIVER

CLINCH RIVER

HOLSTON RIVER

GREAT WAR TRAIL

DAVY CROCKETT
BORN 1786

RIVER

SHERRILL'S

NOLICHUCKY

ABAIR'S

KNOXVILLE
CAVETT

HENRY

FLINT CREEK
BLOODIEST FIGHT - 1789

ROAD

R KILLED
94

792

CAMPBELL'S

GILLESPIE'S
(MASSACRE
1788)

FRENCH BROAD RIVER

TENN.
N.C.

SOUTHWEST POINT

ISH'S

COYATE'S

EASTERN
CHEROKEE
RESERVATION

TELLICO BLOCKHOUSE

GREAT ISLAND
FORT LOUDOUN
TUSKEGEE
TAMOTLEY
TOQUO

CHOTE

CHILHOWIE

KITUWAH

ELLIJAY
BURNING TOWN
AYORE

STICOY

LITTLE TENN. RR.

NATCHEY
TELLICO
CHATUGA

SETTICO

ESTHENORE

COWEE
WATAUGA

TUCKASEGEE

LY'S ISLAND

TASECHEE

NANTAHALA

ETCHOE PASS
MONTGOMERY DEFEATED - 1760

TOCE

HIWASSEE

TAMOTLEY

ETCHOE

MOYEE

HIWASSEE RIVER

CHOTACLOOHEE

OCOEE

IS TALLY

FT. HEMBREE

TENSUNTEE

ESTATOE

AH
UGA

TURTLE TOWN

SPIKE BUCKTOWN

TOXOWAY

RED CLAY

MASSTOWN

STICOYE

USTALLY

QUARATCHIE

DUCKTOWN

NOTALLY

COTHEREE RUTE

TOMASSEE

OCONEE

SUGARTOWN

KEOWEE

FORT PRINCE GEORGE

VANN'S

UNICOY

TALULAH

SOQUEE

NOYOWEE

ELLIJAY

COOSAWATIE

NACOOCHEE

TUGALOO

OOSTANAULA

FROGTOWN

CHOTA

OLD ESTATOE

HASSEE

W ECHOTA
(MOVAL TREATY)
1836

DAHLONEGA

TUSSEE

TURNPIKE

SENECA

TO CHARLESTOWN

TALIWA
(BATTLE - 1755)

LONG SWAMP

SIX'S TOWN
TWO RUNS

WAH
(IER'S LAST FIGHT)
1793

CHATTAHOOCHEE RIVER

TUGALOO R.

KEOWEE

SAVANNAH RIVER

ROSS

THE GEORGIA AND ALABAMA
TOWNS WERE ABANDONED BY THE
CREEKS AFTER THE BATTLE OF
TALIWA IN 1755, AND WERE
OCCUPIED BY THE CHEROKEES
IN THE YEARS FOLLOWING, ESPECIALLY
AFTER THE AMERICAN REVOLUTION
AS THEY WERE COMPELLED TO
CEDE THE MORE NORTHERLY LANDS.

49

A Tragic Alliance

The Indian's alliance with England had an imposing influence in forming the frontiersman's attitude toward the red man. The pioneers were prone to believe that English Agents were inciting all the bloody raids on scattered homes and settlements. In some situations it was only rumor, but the Agent was blamed nevertheless. This type of warfare — the surprise attack, kill, scalp and disappear — was adopted by War Chieftains like Dragging Canoe as the only way they could battle the white man. The atrocities, committed over the country by such tactics, created a permanent hostility in the hearts and minds of the Americans. Such incidents as the massacres in Wyoming Valley of Pennsylvania, the atrocities at Augusta, Georgia, and the killing of the Crockett family at Rogersville, Tennessee, only drew the Patriots closer together and widened the gap between white men and red men.

The Alliance between the Cherokees and the English dates back to 1721. Governor Nicholson of South Carolina invited the Cherokees to a council in Charleston. He wanted to woo the Indian fur trade away from the French traders plying the Mississippi Valley. At the conclusion of the Treaty, the Indians had ceded a fifty square mile tract of land between the Santee, Saluda, and Edisto Rivers. The Treaty also secured a trade agreement with the Cherokees for most of their furs.

Some nine years later Sir Alexander Cuming, taking advantage of the red man's ignorance, pulled off an amazing stunt. This feat influenced the Cherokee Nation for many decades. Cuming, standing outside a Council Hall where some three hundred Indians were meeting, prepared a cunning coup. Concealing guns and a sword under his long coat, he entered the Council Hall. With eloquent words, veiled in threats, he had all the headmen present kneel and swear allegiance to the King of England. To make this stunt creditable he practically forced all the white traders present to sign their names as witnesses. Messengers were then sent into all the towns of the Overhill Country, the Middle Towns, and the Lower Towns. All the Chiefs and headmen were told to meet at Nequassee so many days hence. Cuming planned to have these leaders swear allegiance to the English Crown. (Nequassee was located near present site of Franklin, North Carolina.)

Sir Alexander Cuming had no authority for this performance. He merely seized this course to gain prominence for himself. He dreamed of becoming important as the great benefactor of the red man. He made the grand tour of the Cherokee Nation in his attempt to set up his Kingdom. At Tellico he maneuvered to have Maytoy made Emperor.

From left to right are Ounaconoa, Prince Skalilosken, Kollanna, Oukah Ulah, Tathtowe, Clogoittah, and Ukwaneequa, who became the great Chief Attakullakulla. (From the British Museum.)

Cuming's exploit reached its climax at Nequassee, April 3, 1730. Determined to make all England conscious of his great achievement, he worked out a plan to take several of the young chiefs to London to personally meet the King. The Indians were hesitant about making such an unknown dangerous journey. Finally, seven were persuaded to undertake the long voyage. The Chiefs sailing were Kitagista, Oukahulah, Tiftowe, Clogoitah, Kilonah, Onokanowin, and Oukounaco. The party set sail on His Majesty's Ship, Fox, from Charleston, May 4, 1730.

The arrival of the young Chiefs in London caused quite a commotion. They were wined and dined by the royalty. King George II invited them as guests in the Palace where they were permitted to kiss his hands and those of his two sons. The Chiefs presented to the King their Indian Crown, made of possum fur dyed red, and decorated with scalps and eagle tails. The King paid the expenses of the Indians during their extended trip. Mutual pledges were given by the two nations. The Cherokees promised that no other white people would be allowed to settle in their country, and that they would trade with no one else but King George's representatives. They also promised to aid Great Britain in time of war.

Oukahulah, spokesman for the group, made the following speech as taken from Brown's *Old Frontiers*: "We are come hither from a dark and mountainous country, but we are now in a place of light. The crown of our nation is different from that which our Father, King George, wears, but it is all one. The chain of friendship shall be carried to our people. We look upon King George as the sun, and our Father, and upon ourselves as his children; for though you are white and we are red, our hands and hearts are joined together. When we have acquainted our people with what we have seen, our children from generation to generation will remember it. In war we shall always be as one with you. The great King's enemies shall be our enemies. His people and ours shall always be as one, and we shall die together."

Loaded with presents and honors, the Chiefs returned to their homeland May 11, 1731. The trip and visit consumed an entire year. Sir Alexander Cuming did not return with them because of financial difficulties. The Cherokees had gained a Great White Father but had lost their freedom. The Indian was used by the English, and in the end it was the red man who had to pay.

The Indians watching, as the settlements spread to the northwest and to the southwest, grew more disgruntled. More and more families were moving on his land and building cabins. This land he had won by battle and barter, the land that held the graves of his ancestors. The wilderness, being cut up and destroyed by the whites, furnished his way of life as it would that of his children. He would sign a treaty for so much land, and before he could adjust, another clearing and cabin was springing up on ungranted land. The encroachment moved nearer and nearer to his towns. The Indian could not understand the white man's wanton waste of forests and useless killing of wild animals. His worship of all the elements of nature and its products bordered on the fetish. The varying colors of the four winds governed his life. Every rock, tree, bush, animal, bird and hill contained a spirit that had an influence on his days.

It has been said that the Indian's childlike reasoning and response was indicative of a people emerging from the Stone Age of mind and experince. His desires were immature, his reasoning instinctive rather than the result of thinking. But all races and nationalities have gone, or are going, through various stages of mental development likened to the Stone Age. Thus the white man found the Indian when he landed on the American shores. The big problem was the Indian, an adult in body, could strike back and kill. This made the white man angry.

Then came the fight for freedom and the confusing conflict between people of the same race. The Indians, British allies, fought the Frontiersman from this viewpoint. On the other hand the Settlers, knowing that the Indians were English allies, were confronted with a difficult situation. The international law of having and holding spurred some to argue: "we beat the British; the red men were their allies; to the victor goes the spoils."

The approaching departure of the Overmountain men to battle Ferguson furnished the spark, needed by Agent Cameron, to incite the Cherokees to invade the Nolichucky and Watauga Settlements. While the men were away there would be no one left but the old men, women and children who could easily be captured, killed or driven off their land. "Now is the time," Cameron told the Cherokee-Chickamauga braves. The Agent also told the indian that Ferguson, with his trained British soldiers, would easily defeat the untrained mountaineers. The Indians, believing their White Father, began making plans for a great campaign to regain their lands. They expected little opposition.

The Battle across the mountains was over sooner than Cameron expected and with an entirely different outcome. The British were badly defeated and the Overmountain men back home before the Cherokee-Chickamauga campaign was fully started. The Indians were met at Boyd's Creek and badly defeated. The angry frontiersmen continued on to the Indian towns and burned many of them to the ground. The King's Mountain victory was the beginning of a very bad period for the Cherokee. The land grabbers and territory encroachers really took over. For the Indians it was the beginning of the end.

ROBERT SEVIER

Captain Robert Sevier was mortally wounded at King's Mountain during that final charge up the hill. This was the attack when Sevier's men gained the crest of the ridge and held, giving Shelby and Campbell the flanking support they needed to advance. Robert had stooped to pick up his ramrod from the ground, when a bullet struck him near the kidney. His brother James carried him down the slope to the spring, where he washed and dressed the wound as best he could.

After the Battle, Dr. Uzal Johnson, Tory doctor, tried to extract the bullet but was unable to do so. He treated the wound and advised Robert to lie and rest a few days until the bullet could be taken out safely. Robert insisted upon going home. His reputation as a Tory hater, and the expectation of an attack by Tarleton's forces, did not make King's Mountain a safe place to rest.

With his nephew and other men of his company, he spent the night in the home of John Finley, a Patriot who lived nearby. Joseph Sevier, oldest son of John Sevier, later married Mary Finley of this family.

The four men, James Sevier, Harmon Perryman, William Robertson, and Robert Sevier, left the next day for the Overmountain country and home. Nine days after the battle, at Bright's Place, Captain Robert Sevier became very sick while the men were preparing their meal. He died within an hour.

Robert was wrapped in a blanket and buried in Bright's Cemetery beneath an oak tree. His death occurred the day after the Overmountain men left Quaker Meadows on their return trip across the mountains. The D.A.R. erected a stone in Robert Sevier's honor September 9, 1951. The grave is near Spruce Pine, North Carolina.

TEN WHIGS

Colonel John Moore and some two hundred fifty Tories were camped in a church yard some twenty-five miles from King's Mountain. They were attacked by ten Whigs and completely routed. This event took place either the night before or the night after Ferguson's defeat. Moore's men were a part of Ferguson's returning furloughed soldiers.

The ten Whigs were hiding in the woods, watching the Tories as they were taking what supplies they could find from the Patriot homes along the way. By chance they were able to capture one Tory, and from him learned the location of the planned campsite that night. The Whigs then proceeded to plan a surprise party for the unsuspecting Loyalists.

After dark, the ten Whigs took their posts around the Tory camp. At a given signal they stood up in sight of the Tory guards and gave forth with loud bloodcurdling shouts. The surprised sentries challenged and fired at the attacking force. The Patriots, meanwhile, dropped to the ground and the shots went harmlessly over their heads. Then with loud Indian yells they jumped up, firing their guns as they ran toward the camp. The peaceful evening, the congenial meal, with song and happy campfire atmosphere, were exploded by a desperate fear. Confusion and fright were in complete command. These scared men thought the demons from across the mountains were breathing death and destruction down their backs. Guns, food, clothing and everything else were forgotten in their hurry to escape into the safety of darkness. The entire force, officers and privates, fled in terrified haste and from all reports kept traveling.

The ten Whigs cautiously entered the campsite. Not one Tory was present. With the extra captured guns loaded and by their side, they stood guard all night, expecting a Loyalist attack every moment. When dawn arrived, they packed the supplies into wagons, hitched the fifteen captured horses up and carried the food and other needed items back home. It is said they divided with their needy neighbors.

CAPTAINS JOHN WEIR and ROBERT SHANNON, living in the vicinity of King's Mountain, had heard of the Patriot force marching to do battle with the Tories. They had summoned their men and moved forth to join them in the fight. They might have arrived too late to join in the actual battle, but it can be assumed that they assisted in every way possible in attending wounded, guarding prisoners and other chores that would give the tired fighters some relief.

Pictured are suits of clothing worn by Greer. They hang in the Tennessee State Museum, Nashville, Tennessee. Pictures of Greer's clothing and Sevier's Sword and Gun by courtesy Fred Estes, director of the state museum.

The King's Mountain Messenger

Soon after the King's Mountain victory Joseph Greer was dispatched, by Colonel John Sevier, to carry news of the Battle to Congress assembled in Philadelphia.

Young Greer, twenty years old and over seven feet tall, was armed with a musket and compass for the long dangerous trip. Many reasons can be conjectured as to why Sevier selected Greer for this particular mission. The important one was Greer's knowledge of the Indians. For years Joseph had traveled with his father among the Indian towns. Andrew Greer, a Scotsman, had traded with the red men from the moment he arrived in the new country. Another good reason, it would take an experienced woodsman to plot his way through the forests and Tory settlements. All this experience proved valuable to young Greer as he journeyed north.

Joseph Greer had one or more horses shot from under him by the Indians. Much of the trip had to be covered on foot. He had to swim several streams, some covered by ice. One night was spent in a big hollow log, hiding from a party of braves who had been following him all day. From his concealment in the log, he could hear them talking as they tried to pick up his trail. It is said that they actually sat on the log for a spell.

On Greer's arrival in Philadelphia, he made his way to Congressional Headquarters. The doorkeeper tried to bar his entrance. The giant messenger pushed him aside, stalked down the aisle, and delivered his message to a surprised body of men. It is said that General Washington commented: "With soldiers like him, no wonder the frontiersmen won."

Joseph Greer was given a grant of three thousand acres for this service and other participation during the fight for independence. The tract was located in what is now Lincoln County, Tennessee. Greer acquired several bordering tracts until his holdings covered some ten thousand acres. It is said that you could ride a straight line all day and not get off Greer land. The Greer Clan has many descendants living in Cane Creek Valley.

SWORD AND PISTOL PRESENTED TO COLONEL JOHN SEVIER

The General Assembly of North Carolina, during the first session after the King's Mountain victory, passed a resolution that a sword and pistol should be presented to both Colonel John Sevier and Colonel Isaac Shelby for the great service they had given their country. This session of the Assembly met in Halifax, January 18, 1781.

On one side of the sword handle, presented to Colonel Sevier, is engraved "State of North Carolina to Colonel John Sevier," and on the other side, "King's Mountain, October 7, 1780." The sword and pistol, in photograph on preceding page, were inherited by Colonel George Washington Sevier and given by him to the State of Tennessee.

Though this resolution was adopted in 1781, the swords and pistols were not delivered until 1813. North Carolina Governor William Hawkins wrote a letter to Sevier with apologies for the oversight. These historic reminders of King's Mountain are in the State Museum at Nashville, Tennessee. Swords and pistols were also presented to other commanding officers.

COLONEL PATRICK FERGUSON

(This list of officers very limited. Space and time did not allow a fuller roster.)

Killed (k)   Hanged (h)   Wounded (w)

Captain Abraham De Peyster
  (Second in command)
Captain Alexander Chesney *(Left Diary)*
Colonel Ambrose Mills (h)
Major _____ Lee
Major Daniel Plummer (k)
Major William Mills
Captain Samuel Ryerson (w)
Captain John McGinnis
Captain Aron Bickerstaff
  (Mortally wounded. Trial and hanging took place on his farm.)
Colonel Vesey Husbands (k)
Captain William Gist
Captain William Green

Captain _____ Wilson (h)
Captain James Chittwood (h)
Captain _____ Grimes (h)
Captain _____ Towsend
Captain Walter Gilkey (h)

Aid-de-Camp Elias Powell
Lieutenant William Langum
Lieutenant John Taylor
Lieutenant Anthony Allaire
  (Wrote diary)
Lieutenant William Stevenson
Lieutenant Duncan Fletcher
Lieutenant John McGinnis (k)
Lieutenant _____ Lafferty (h)

Privates: John McFall (h), John Bebby (h), Augustine Hobbs (h).

Major Patrick Ferguson was born in Aberdeen, Scotland. His father, Lord Pitfour, had restored the family fortune to the extent that he was able to afford a good family background for his children. Young Patrick began an early education, but hunting and soldiering appealed more than the academic. His family purchased a commission for him at the age of fifteen. He entered active service with the Royal North Dragoons, July 12, 1759. Although of small body frame, young Ferguson was serious-minded and had sound judgment and abundant energy.

After years of experience, excepting six of sickness, Captain Ferguson was sent to America in 1777. He soon had a reputation as one of the best marksmen in the country. During the first three years he saw action in the New England battles. He was sent to South Carolina when the invasion started at Charleston. Here he was given the temporary rank of Lieutenant-Colonel. Ferguson had received a wound in his right arm during the Battle of Brandywine, making it almost useless the rest of his life.

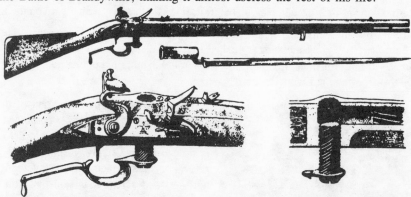

Pictured here is the first successful breech loading rifle which was developed by Patrick Ferguson. One of these guns hangs in the Museum at King's Mountain. Pictures by courtesy of King's Mountain National Military Park personnel.

KING'S MOUNTAIN SOLDIERS

An incomplete listing of the officers and men that participated in the King's Mountain Campaign

Rank listed is at time of battle. (k) killed, (w) wounded, (?) no proof

Allen, Richard, Captain
(stayed with footsoldiers)
Anderson, Gerorge, Major
Anderson, John Jr., Lieutenant
Andrews, John, Lieutenant
Arbunkle, Mathew, Captain

Barnes, Alexander, Captain
Bartlett, William, Lieutenant
Barnett, Alexander, Captain
Barton, John, Captain
Barry, Andrew, Captain
Beattie, John, Lieutenant (k)
Beattie, William, Captain
Beattie, David, Captain
Bean, Jesse, Captain
Bean, William, Captain
Beverly, John, Captain
Blacock, Samuel G., Major
Blackburn, William, Lieutenant (k)
Blackmore, William, Lieutenant
Bishop, Levi, Lieutenant
Boyd, John, Lieutenant
Bowen, William, Captain
Bowen, Arthur, Captain
Bowen, Reese, Lieutenant
Brandon, Thomas, Colonel
Brandon, John, Captain
Boran, Baile, Lieutenant
Bradshear, Samuel, Captain
Bradshear, Robert, Captain
Breckenridge, Alexander, Captain
Breckenridge, Robert, Captain
Brown, Jacob, Captain
Brown, John, Captain
Brown, Andrew, Captain
Buckner, Joshua, Lieutenant
Black, Joseph, Lieutenant

Caldwell, Samuel, Captain
Caldwell, Thomas, Captain
Callahan, John, Captain
Callahan, Joel, Lieutenant
Campbell, William, Colonel
(Commander-in-Chief)
Campbell, John, Captain
Campbell, Robert, Lieutenant
Campbell, Patrick, Lieutenant
Campbell, Hugh, Lieutenant
Caruthers, Andrew, Lieutenant
Candler, William, Major
Carr, Paddy, Captain
Carter, Landon, Lieutenant
Carson, John, Captain
Christian, Gilbert, Major
Chronicle, William, Major (k)
Clark, John, Captain
Cleveland, Benjamin, Colonel
Cleveland, John, Lieutenant
Cleveland, Larkin, Lieutenant
(wounded enroute to King's Mountain)

Cloud, Joseph, Captain
Cowan, Andrew, Captain
Cowan, William, Captain
Corry, James, Lieutenant (k)
Condley, John, Captain
Colville, Andrew, Captain
Coulter, John, Captain
Cox, William, Captain
Craig, David, Captain
Craig, Robert, Captain
Crabtree, James, Captain
Crockett, Joseph, Captain
Crockett, Walter, Major
Crockett, William, Lieutenant
Crockett, Joseph, Captain
Crow, John, Captain

Davenport, William, Colonel
Davis, John, Captain
Davis, Andrew, Lieutenant
Davison, William, Lieutenant
Davison, Daniel, Lieutenant
Daugherty, George, Captain
Dickson, Joseph, Major
Dillard, James, Captain
Dryden, Nathaniel, Lieutenant (k)
Dysart, James, Captain (w)
Duff, William, Captain

Edmondson, William, Major
Edmondson, William, Captain (k)
Edmondson, Robert Sr., Captain (k)
Edmondson, Robert Jr., Lieutenant (w)
Edmondson, Andrew, Captain (k)
Elliot, James, Captain
Espey, Samuel, Captain (w)
Ewing, Alexander, Captain

Fapolson, Andrew, Captain
Fear, Edmond, Captain
Franklin, John, Captain
Franklin, Jesse, Captain
Forney, Peter, Captain
Fulkerson, James, Captain

Gilliespie, Thomas, Captain
Gilliespie, William, Captain
Gillilland, James, Lieutenant
Gilreath, William, Captain
Gist, Benjamin, Captain
Goff, Andrew, Lieutenant
Gordan, Charles, Major
Gray, William, Lieutenant

Hadley, Joshua, Captain
Hampton, Andrew, Colonel
Hambright, Frederick, Lieutenant-Colonel
Hambright, John, Lieutenant
Hannah, Robin, Captain
Hammond, Samuel, Major

KING'S MOUNTAIN SOLDIERS

Harvey, John, Captain
Hawthorne, James, Lieutenant-Colonel
Hayes, Joseph, Colonel
  (succeeded to Gen. Williams' command)
Handley, Samuel, Captain
Hemphill, Thomas, Captain
Herndon, Benjamin, Lieutenant-Colonel
Herndon, Joseph, Major
  (remained with footsoldiers)
Hickman, James, Captain
Hill, William, Colonel
  (in command of Sumpter's force)
Hollis, John, Captain
Houston, James, Ensign
Houston, John, Ensign
Hughes, Joseph, Lieutenant

Isbell, Godfrey, Captain
Isbell, Zachery, Lieutenant

Jack, James, Captain
Jackson, William, Captain
Jamison, John, Lieutenant
Jernigan, George, Lieutenant
Johnson, James, Major
Johnson, John, Captain
Johnson, Samuel, Captain
Johnson, James, Captain
Johnson, Samuel, Lieutenant (w)
Johnston, William, Captain

Kennedy, Robert, Captain

Lacey, Edward, Colonel
  (commanded the Sumpter force during battle)
Lenoir, William, Captain (w)
Leeper, James, Lieutenant
Lewis, James Martin, Lieutenant (w)
Lewis, Joel, Captain (w)
Lewis, Aron, Captain
Lewis, Micajah, Major (w)
Lewis, Joel, Lieutenant (w)
Litton, Solomon, Lieutenant
Looney, David, Captain
Looney, Moses, Lieutenant
Lowery, John, Lieutenant
Love, Andrew, Colonel
Love, William, Lieutenant
Lucas, Isaac, Captain
Lucas, Joseph, Captain
Lucas, Robert, Captain
Lusk, Joseph, Captain
Lytte, Thomas, Captain
Lyon, Huberson, Lieutenant (k)
Lane, Isaac, Lieutenant
Ledbetter, George, Captain

McDowell, Charles, Colonel
McDowell, Joseph, Major
  *(commanded his brother Charles' force
  during battle)*
McDowell, Joseph, Captain
  (cousin)

McCullock, Thomas, Lieutenant (k)
McCutchan, Samuel, Captain
McFarland, Robert, Lieutenant
McFerrin, John, Ensign
McKissick, David, Captain
McNabb, David, Captain
Mattox, Charles, Lieutenant
Mattox, John, Captain (k)
Martin, George, Lieutenant
Martin, Samuel, Captain
Maxwell, George, Captain
Meek, Adam, Lieutenant
Meredith, William, Captain
Miller, James, Captain
Moffett, John, Captain
Montgomery, James, Captain

Neal, William, Captain
  (stayed with footsoldiers)
Newell, Samuel, Lieutenant (w)
Nixon, John, Captain

Oglesby, William, Captain

Pemberton, John, Captain
Phillips, James, Lieutenant (k)
Pittman, William, Lieutenant
Porter, James, Major
Preston, Thomas, Captain

Rabb, William, Lieutenant
Rains, John, Captain
Reynolds, Elisha, Lieutenant
Riggs, Bethial
Robinson, William, Lieutenant
Robinson, John, Lieutenant
Roseborough, William, Captain
Russell, George, Lieutenant
Russell, Andrew, Captain
Russell, William, Lieutenant

Sample, Samuel, Captain
Sawyers, John, Captain
Sevier, John, Colonel
Sevier, Valentine, Major
Sevier, Robert, Captain
  (mortally wounded)
Sevier, Valentine, Captain
Scott, Joseph Sr., Lieutenant
Shannon, Robert, Captain
Sharp, Thomas, Lieutenant
Shelby, Isaac, Colonel
Shelby, John, Captain
Shelby, Evan Jr., Major
Shelby, Moses, Captain
Sigmon, John, Captain
Singleton, Andrew, Captain
Singleton, Richard, Major
Smith, Henry, Captain
Smith, William, Captain
Smith, Henry, Captain
Smith, Miner, Captain (w)
Smith, Daniel, Captain
Smith, J.M., Lieutenant

KING'S MOUNTAIN SOLDIERS

Snoddy, John, Captain
Steen, James, Colonel (k)
Steele, John, Lieutenant
Stinson, James, Captain
Syles, James, Captain

Taylor, Christopher, Captain
Tate, Samuel, Major
Thompson, John, Captain
Thompson, James, Captain
Tipton, Jonathan, Major
Tipton, William, Lieutenant
Trimble, Robert, Captain
Trimble, William, Captain
Topp, Roger, Captain

Vance, David, Captain
Vance, John, Lieutenant
Vanhook, Samuel, Lieutenant

Wallace, Andrew, Captain
Walker, Felix, Lieutenant-Colonel
Walton, Jesse, Major
Watson, Patrick, Major
(stayed with footsoldiers)
Webb, David, Captain
Weir, John, Captain
Weir, Samuel, Captain
White, Thomas, Lieutenant
White, Isaac, Captain
White, Richard, Lieutenant
White, Joseph, Captain
Witherspoon, David, Lieutenant
Wilson, Zacheus, Captain
Withrow, James, Captain
Williams, James, Colonel (k)
Williams, Joseph, Captain
Williams, Samuel, Captain
Wilson, Joseph, Captain
Wiley, Alexander, Lieutenant
Willoughby, William, Lieutenant
Wood, Samuel, Captain
Womach, Jacob, Captain

Abernathy, Robert
Adams, John
Adams, William
Alexander, Daniel
Alexander, Elias
Alexander, James
Alexander, Jerimiah
Alexander, John
Alexander, Oliver
Allen, Moses
Allen, Richard
Allen, Vincent
Allison, John (w)
Alston, William
Anderson, Jacob
Anderson, James
Anderson, John
Anderson, William
Applegate, Thomas
Arbuckle, Thomas
Arbuckle, Mathew
Armstrong, Robert
Armstrong, James
Armstrong, Isaac
Armstrong, Mathew
Armstrong, William
Avender, Andrew
Axer, Sam

Blackwell, David
Bacon, Michael
Baker, John
Bakly, Charles
Balch, Amos
Ballew, Richard
Banning, Benoni (w)
Barker, Charles
Barker, Edmond
Barker, Edward

Barker, Enoch
Barker, Joel
Barker, Henry
Barnes, Alexander
Barnes, Benjamin (?)
Barnes, Shadrack (?)
Barnett, Alexander
Bartlett, William
Barton, Benjamin
Barton, John
Barton, Joshua
Barton, Isaac
Barry, Andrew
Bean, George
Bean, Jesse
Bean, John
Bean, Robert
Beard, Robert
Bearden, Jeremiah
Bearden, John
Beattie, David
Beattie, John (k)
Beattie, Francis
Beattie, William
Beeler, Jacob
Beeler, Joseph
Bell, Samuel
Bell, Thomas
Bell, William
Bennedict, John
Bentley, John
Berry, Bradley
Berry, James
Berry, Thomas
Berry, Andrew
Berry, Robert
Besall, John
Bickley, Summers
Bickley, Charles

Bicknell, James
Bicknell, Thomas (k)
Bingham, Benjamin
Biffle, Jacob
Bishop, Levi
Black, Joseph
Blackburn, Arthur
Blackburn, George
Blackburn, Joseph
Blackburn, Robert
Blackburn, John
Blackburn, William (k)
Blackmore, John
Blackmore, William
Blalock, Samuel
Blassingham, John
Blair, James
Blair, John
Blevin, Henry
Blevin, Daniel
Blyth, Thomas
Bolling, Jerry
Boran, Bazi
Boren, John
Bowen, Charles
Bowen, John
Bowen, Henry
Bowers, Leonard
Bowman, Esaius
Bowman, Sparkling
Box, Samuel
Boyer, Thomas (k)
Boyd, William
Boyd, John (k)
Boyce, John
Bradley, William (w)
Bradley, Richard
Brandon, Mathew
Brazelton, William

KING'S MOUNTAIN SOLDIERS

Brakshears, Mattis
Breckenridge, Alexander
Breckenridge, George
Breckenridge, John
Breden, John
Britt, Obediah
Briggs, John
Brimer, William
Brigham, James
Brooks, George
Brooks, Thomas
Brooks, John
Brooks, William
Brooks, David
Brooks, Moses
Broom, W. M.
Brown, John (k)
Brown, James
Brown, Low
Brown, John S. C.
Brown, Thomas
Brown, Stephen
Brown, Isaiah
Brown, Peter
Brown, George
Brown, Joseph
Brown, Michael
Browning, Enos
Bruster, E. (?)
Brush, Enoch
Buchanan, Samuel
Buchanan, Robert
Buchanan, Alexander
Budvine, Francis
Bullen, William (w)
Bullen, Isaac
Bullen, Luke
Burney, William
Burney, Simon
Burns, Laird
Burns, William

Caldwell, Samuel
Caldwell, William
Callahan, Joel
Callahan, John
Callaway, Elijah
Callaway, Richard
Callaway, William
Camp, Thomas
Camp, Nathan
Camp, Thomas
Camp, John
Camp, Benjamin
Camp, Edmund
Campbell, Joseph
Campbell, David
Campbell, William Jr.
Campbell, Robert (w)
Campbell, Hugh
Campbell, James
Campbell, Jeremiah
Campbell, Patrick
Candler, Henry
Cantrell, Stephen

Carmichal, John
Carmack, Cornelius
Carmack, John
Carpenter, John
Carr, Patrick
Carrol, William
Carson, Andrew
Carson, David
Carson, John
Carson, William
Carwell, Alexander
Carswell, John
Cartwright, Joseph
Carathurs, James
Cardwell, Perrin
Carter, Charles
Casewell, Zadrack
Casey, Benjamin
Casey, Levi
Casey, Randolph
Casey, William
Cash, David
Cathcart, Joseph
Castillo, John
Caunice, Nicholas
Chambers, Robert
Chapman, John
Chapman, Benjamin
Cheney, Thomas
Childers, John (w)
Childress, Mitchell
Childress, Thomas
Chisholm, John
Childress, Mitchell
Childress, William
Childress, John
Chittim, John (w)
Chitwood, James
Christian, George (?)
Clark, George
Clark, Michael
Clark, William
Clark, James
Clay, William
Clayborn, John
Clem, William
Cleveland, Ezekiel
Cleveland, Robert
Clon, William
Clowney, Samuel
Cloa, Willis
Cobb, Arthur
Cobb, Jerry
Cobb, Pharoh
Cobb, William Sr.
Cobb, William Jr.
Cockrell, John (?)
Cole, Joseph
Cole, Thomas
Cole, William
Colley, Daniel
Colley, Thomas
Collins, James
Collins, Samuel
Coleman, Spense

Collinworth, John
Colvill, Joseph
Colville, Samuel (w)
Compton, Jeremiah
Cook, William
Cook, Charles
Cook, Edward
Cook, Robert
Cook, Elisha
Coop, Horatia
Cope, John
Copeland, Zacheus
Corry, James (k)
Cosby, James
Costner, Thomas
Coulter, Martin
Coultrie, Robert
Covey, Samuel
Cowan, David
Cowan, James
Cowan, Andrew
Cowan, William
Cowan, Samuel
Cowan, Nathaniel
Cowan, Thomas
Cox, Charles
Cox, James
Cox, Curd
Cox, William (w)
Craig, Robert
Craig, David
Craig, James
Craig, John
Crawford, Charles
Crawford, John
Crawford, John
Crenshaw, John
Creswell, Andrew
Crock, William
Crockett, William
Crockett, Samuel
Crockett, John
Cross, Joseph
Cross, Elijah
Cross, Zachrack (?)
Crow, James
Crow, John
Crumbless, Thomas
Crunk, William
Culbertson, Josiah
Culbertson, Robert
Cummings, Andrew
Cunningham, Jonathan
Curry, James
Cusick, John
Cusick, George
Cutbirth, Andrew

Dalton, John
Dameron, George
Darnell, David (w)
Darnell, Cornelius
Darnell, Lawrence
David, Azariah

KING'S MOUNTAIN SOLDIERS

Dave, Thomas
Davidson, Benjamin
Davidson, William
Davidson, Samuel
Davidson, Daniel
Davis, John
Davis, Nathaniel
Davis, Robert
Davis, Samuel
Davis, William
Davis, Joel
Davis, Nathan
Dawson, Elias
Deatheridge, John
Delaney, William
Dennison, Robert
Depew, Isaac
Desha, Robert
Detgaoorett, John
Dickinson, Henry
Dickey, Andrew
Dickey, David
Dillard, Benjamin
Dillard, James
Dixon, Joseph
Dixon, John
Dixon, Joel
Doaling, Robert
Doherty, George Sr.
Dobkins, Jacob
Dobson, Robert
Dodd, William
Dobson, Joseph
Donald, James
Dolberry, Lytton
Doran, Alexander
Doran, James
Doran, Terence
Dorton, Moses
Dorton, William Jr,
Douglas, James
Douglas, Johnathan (w)
Douglas, Robert
Douglas, Edward
Dryden, James
Dryden, Nathaniel (k)
Dryden, William
Duck, Samuel
Duckworth, John
Duff, David (k)
Duff, Samuel
Dunn, Samuel
Dunn, William
Duncan, Jesse
Duncan, Joseph
Duncan, John
Duncan, Thomas
Dunlop, James
Dysart, John

Eaken, William
Earnest, Earnest
Earnest, Rev. Felix
Eddleman, Peter
Edgman, William

Edmiston, Samuel
Edmiston, John
Edmiston, Thomas
Edmiston, Robert
Edmiston, William
Elder, Robert
Elmore, William
Ely, William
Enlow, Potter
England, John
England, Joseph
Estill, Benjamin
Evans, Andrew
Evans, Ardin
Evans, David
Evans, Evan
Evans, Samuel
Evans, Phillip
Everett, William
Ewart, James
Ewart, Robert
Ewing, George
Ewin, Hugh
Fagan, John (w)
Fain, Samuel
Fain, Nicholas
Farewell, James
Farewell, John
Faris, Thomas
Faris, Isaac
Faris, John
Faris, Larkin
Faris, Martin
Faris, Richard
Farrow, Landon
Farrow, Samuel
Farrow, Thomas
Farrow, John
Fear, Thomas
Fear, Edmond
Feimster, William
Findley, John
Findley, George
Fisher, Frederick (w)
Fitch, John
Fleenor, Charles
Fleenor, Michael
Fleenor, Joel
Flemming, John
Fletcher, Thomas
Floyd, Andrew
Floyd, John
Flower, William (w)
Folson, Andrew
Ford, John
Fork, William
Fork, Peter
Forney, Abraham
Forrister, Robert
Fowler, William (k)
Fowler, John
Fowler, James
Fox, John
Francis, Thomas
Frazer, David

Frazer, Daniel
Frazer, John
Frazier, Samuel
Freeman, William
Freeland, James
Frierson, Robert
Frierson, William
Frierson, Thomas
Frierson, James
Frierson, John
Frigge, John
Frigge, J. C.
Frigge, Robert
Frost, Micajah
Fulkerson, Richard
Fulkerson, John
Fulkerson, James
Fulkner, David
Furgason, James

Gaines, James Sr.
Gaines, James
Gaines, Ambrose
Galbreath, Arthur
Galbreath, Robert (?)
Galbreath, John (?)
Galliher, John
Galliher, Joel
Galloway, Alexander
Gamble, Robert
Gamble, Choat
Gamble, Josiah
Gammon, Harris
Gann, Thomas
Garner, John
Gaspenson, John
Gass, John
Gaston, William
Geren, Solomon
Gervis, James
Gibson, John
Gibson, Thomas
Gibbs, Nicholas
Giles, William (w)
Gilleland, John (w)
Gillespie, James
Gillespie, Jacob
Gillespie, Thomas
Gillespie, George
Gilliam, Devereux
Gilmer, Enoch
Gilmer, William (w)
Gist, Joseph
Gist, Joshua
Gist, Nathaniel (k)
Gist, Richard
Gist, Thomas
Given, James
Given, John
Glenn, John
Godwin, Joseph
Godwin, Robinson
Godwin, Samuel
Goforth, Preston (k)
Goff, Andrew

KING'S MOUNTAIN SOLDIERS

Goff, William
Goodman, Henry
Gordon, Charles (w)
Gordon, Chapman
Gordon, George
Gorsage, John
Gourley, Thomas
Graham, James
Graham, William
Graves, Boston
Gray, James
Gray, Jessee
Grantham, Richard
Green, Jesse
Greenlee, James
Greever, Phillip
Greer, Alexander
Greer, Andrew
Greer, William
Greer, Andrew Jr.
Greer, Joseph
Gregory, John
Grier, John
Grier, James
Griffith, Joseph
Grimes, George
Grimes, James
Guest, Moses
Gwaltney, Nathan

Hackett, John
Hadden, George
Hager, Simon
Haile, John
Hale, William
Hale, Lewis
Hall, David
Hall, John
Hall, Thomas
Hall, Jesse
Hambright, John Hardin
Hamby, William
Hamer, James
Hamilton, Alexander
Hamilton, Joshua
Hamilton, Thomas
Hamilton, John
Hamilton, Robert
Hammond, Charles
Hampton, Edward
Hampton, Jonathan
Hampton, Andrew
Hampton, John
Hampton, Joel
Handly, Robert
Handly, Samuel
Hanna, Robert
Hanna, Andrew
Hancock, Stephen
Hancock, Joseph
Hank, Michael
Hankins, Abraham
Hansley, Robert
Handy, Thomas
Hardeman, Thomas

Hardin, Abraham
Hardin, Joseph Jr.
Hardin, John
Harkleroad, Henry
Harlison, Herndon
Harrell, Reuben
Harrell, John (?)
Harrell, Joseph (?)
Harrell, Kidder
Harris, James
Harrison, Gideon
Harrison, Nathaniel
Harmison, John
Harper, Richard
Hart, Leonard
Harwood, William
Hays, Samuel
Hayter, Israel (w)
Hedrick, William
Helms, John
Helm, Meredith (?)
Helton, Abraham
Hemphill, Charles
Henderson, John
Henderson, Daniel
Henderson, Joseph
Henderson, Robert
Henderson, William
Henderson, John
Hendrick, David
Hendrick, Solomon
Hendrick, Moses
Henegar, Henry (k)
Henegar, Jacob
Henegar, John
Henniger, Conrad
Henry, Henry
Henry, James
Henery, Moses (k)
Henry, John (k)
Henry, Joseph
Henry, Henry
Henry, Robert (w)
Henry, Samuel
Henry, Hugh
Henry, William
Hensley, Samuel
Hereden, James
Hereden, Edward
Hickman, James
Hickman, Joel
Hickman, Thomas
Higgins, John
Higgenbottom, Robert
Hill, James
Hillian, James
Hillian, John
Hobbs, Thomas
Hoffman, Jacob
Hoffman, John
Hotchkiss, Jared
Holloway, Charles
Holloway, John
Holloway, Benjamin
Hollingsworth, Benjamin

Holdway, Timothy
Holland, Isaac Jr.
Hood, John
Hortenstine, Abraham
Horton, Daniel (?)
Horton, Henry
Horton, Joshua (?)
Horton, John
Horton, Zephaniah (?)
Houston, William
Houston, John
Houston, James
Housley, Robert
Houghton, Thomas
Howard, William
Hubbard, James
Hudson, John
Hufacre, George
Hughes, David
Hughes, Peter
Hughes, Francis
Hughes, Thomas
Hundley, Samuel
Hunter, Thomas
Hyce, Leonard (w)
Hyden, William
Hyder, Michael

Ingle, John
Inglis, Michael
Ingram, Jeremiah
Inman, Abednego (w)
Ireland, Hans
Isaac, Samuel
Isbell, James
Isbell, Francis
Isbell, Livington
Isbell, Thomas
Isbell, Zackary
Isbell, Henry (?)
Ivy, Henry

Jack, James
Jack, Jerimiah
Jack, Patrick (?)
Jackson, Churchwell
James, John
James, Rolling
James, Marlin
Jamison, Samuel
Jamison, John
Jamison, Thomas
Jamison, Robert
Jarnigan, George
Jefferies, John
Jefferies, Nathaniel
Jefferies, Jean
Jefferies, Phillip
Jefferies, Nathan
Jenkins, Jacob
Jenkins, Thomas
Jenkins, William
Jenkins, James
Jennings, David
Jernigan, Thomas

KING'S MOUNTAIN SOLDIERS

Jernigan, William
Johnson, James S.
Johnson, Barnett
Johnson, John
Johnson, Robert
Johnson, Peter
Johnson, Samuel (w)
Jones, Daniel
Jones, David
Jones, James
Jones, John
Jones, Joseph
Jones, Joshua (w)
Judd, John
Judd, Rowland

Karr, Robert
Karr, Mathew
Keeps, James
Keele, Richard S.
Kelly, John
Kelley, William
Kendrick, Benjamin
Kendrick, Samuel
Kendrick, John
Kendricks, Solomon
Kennedy, Daniel
Kennedy, John
Kennedy, Thomas
Kennedy, Moses
Kennedy, William
Kennedy, Robert
Kendred, Thomas
Kerby, Henry
Kerr, Adam
Kerr, Joseph
Keys, James
Keys, Mathew
Kidd, John
Kilgore, Charles (w)
Kilgore, William
Kilgore, Hiram
Kilgore, James
Kilgore, Robert (w)
King, Robert
King, John
King, William
King, Andrew
Kincannon, Andrew
Kincannon, James
Kincannon, Mathew
Kindle, William
Kinkead, John
Kitchen, John
Knox, Robert
Knox, Benjamin (?)
Knox, Samuel
Knox, James (?)
Kuykendall, Mathew
Kuykendall, Benjamin
Kuykendall, Joseph

Laird, David
Laird, James (k)
Laird, John (k)
Lane, Isaac

Lane, Richard
Lane, Tidence
Lane, Aquilla
Lane, William
Lane, Jesse
Lane, Charles
Lane, James
Lane, John
Lane, Samuel
Landrum, James
Landrum, Thomas
Langston, John
Langston, Robert
Lankford, John
Lankford, Benjamin
Lannim, Joseph
Large, Joseph
Larrimore, Hugh
Lathan, John
Latman, Joseph
Lawson, William
Lay, Thomas
Lawson, John
Lee, James
Leeper, Samuel
Leeper, James
Leffy, Shadrack
Lengley, William
Leonard, George
Leonard, Frederick
Leonard, Henry
Leonard, Robert (?)
Lenoir, William
Lesley, Thomas
Lewallen, Michael
Lewis, James
Lewis, John
Lewis, Aron
Lewis, William Terrill
Lewis, Charles
Lindsay, James
Lindsay, John
Linn, Andrew
Linn, Daniel
Linn, William
Limonton, Robert
Litton, Catel
Litton, John
Liles, David
Liture, Harmon
Livingston, David
Logan, Joseph
Logan, William
Logan, James
Long, John
Long, William
Long, Richard
Long, Robert
Long, Nicholas
Love, Robert
Love, John
Love, Hezekiah
Looney, Robert
Looney, John
Lowery, John

Lowery, William
Loyd, John
Lyle, Henry
Lyle, Samuel
Lynn, David
Lynn, Adam
Lyon, Humberson
Lyon, William
Lytle, Archibald
Lytle, Micajah
Lytle, William
Lyman, Jacob
Lusk, William (k)
Lusk, Joseph
Lusk, Hugh

McAden, William
McAdoo, John
McBee, Silas
McBee, Israel
McCarthy, William
McCallister, William
McCallon, James
McCampbell, Solomon
McClelland, Abraham
McClelland, John
McClough, James
McClure, John
McConnell, Abram
McCormick, Thomas
McCormick, Joseph
McCormick, Robert
McCorkle, Francis
McCoy, Robert
McCroy, Mathew
McCroskey, John
McCulloch, John
McCutcheon, William
McCutcheon, Samuel
McCutcheon, John
McCulloch, Robert (w)
McCulloch, Thomas (k)
McDonald, Magnus
McElwee, James
McElwee, John
McElwee, William
McFarland, Robert
McFerrin, John
McFerrin, Martin
McGaughey, Samuel
McHenry, John
McJucken, Joseph
McKamey, James
McGrill, James
McGill, John
McKee, James
McKisnick, Thomas
McLain, Thomas
McLain, Alexander
McMaster, William
McLemore, John
McMillan, Alexander
McMillan, William
McMillan, Joseph
McNabb, John

KING'S MOUNTAIN SOLDIERS

McNelly, John
McNutt, Alexander
McNutt, George
McPeters, Joseph
McQueen, James
McShaney, William
McSpadden, William
McWheeler, Andrew
Madonough, Andrew
Mahannas, Taploy
Mahoney, Nichael (k)
Main, Tobias
Main, Henry
Malaby, John
Manley, Amos
Manor, Josiah
Manor, Thomas
Mason, William
Maples, Marmaduke
Martin, Samuel
Martin, Salathiel
Martin, John
Martin, Robert
Martin, William
Martin, Mathew
Marshall, Marcum
Marney, Amos
Mason, Patrick
Mason, James
Mason, Thomas
Mason, Edward
Massingale, Henry
Massingale, Michael
Massingale, James
Mathews, James
Mattox, Charles
Maxwell, John
Maxwell, James
Maxwell, Thomas
May, Cassimore
May, Humphrey
May, John
Mayes, Samuel
Mayes, William
Meaden, Andrew
Meaden, John
Meek, John
Meek, Adam
Meek, Moses
Meek, James
Mendenhall, Nathan
Metcalf, William
Miller, John
Miller, Robert (w)
Miller, John H.
Miller, Martin
Millen, John
Millon, Anthony
Miliken, James
Mitchel, James
Mitchel, Elijah
Mitchel, Edward
Moffett, John
Monroe, William
Montgomery, Alexander
Montgomery, James

Montgomery, Richard
Montgomery, Robert
Montgomery, Thomas
Mooney, Martin
Mooney, Richard
Moore, Alexander
Moore, Thomas
Moore, John
Moore, Alexander
Moore, James
Moore, William (w)
Moore, Samuel
Moore, William
Moorehead, John
Morgan, Isaac
Morrison, Peter
Morrison, William
Mosier, Francis
Moser, Abraham
Murdoch, John
Munday, Jeremiah
Murphy, Patrick (w)
Murphy, William
Murphy, Joseph
Murphee, Henry
Murphee, John
Musick, Lewis

Nave, Abraham
Nave, Conrad
Nave, Henry
Nave, Teeler
Neal, John
Neal, Zephaniah
Neally, B.
Neally, William
Nelson, John
Nelson, Sutney
Nelson, William
Newell, Samuel Sr.
Newell, Samuel Jr.
Newman, Isaac
Newman, Jacob
Newman, John
Newland, Lewis
Newland, Abram
Newland, Isaac
Newton, Benjamin
Nicholas, Flayl
Nicholas, James
Norton, Alexander
Norman, William
Nuanly, Henry

O'Brien, William
Oglesby, Elisha
O'Gullion, Barney
O'Gullion, Hugh
Oliver, Dionysius
Oliphant, John
Outlaw, Alexander
Overton, Eli
Owen, John
Owen, Robert

Palmer, John

Palmer, Peter
Palmer, Thomas
Panter, Adam
Parke, Ezekial
Parke, George
Parke, Henry
Parke, George
Parker, Humphrey
Patterson, Arthur (k)
Patterson, Arthur Jr.
Patterson, Thomas
Patterson, Robert
Patterson, John
Patterson, William
Patterson, William (k)
Parry, John
Patton, Robert
Patton, Jacob
Pearce, Joshua
Peck, Adam
Peeber, Silas
Peek, Able
Peek, Adam
Peden, John
Pendergast, Garrett
Pendergrass, Alexander
Penland, Robert
Pemberton, John
Pepper, Elisha (k)
Perkins, Elisha
Perrin, Joseph
Perry, Richard
Perry, Solomon
Perry, Jesse
Perryman, Harmon
Pertle, George
Peters, William
Phillips, James
Phillips, Samuel
Phillips, Joseph
Pierce, Joseph
Pilcher, Robert
Piper, James
Pippin, Robert
Pittman, William
Pitts, Louis
Plunk, Jacob
Polk, Ezekial
Pollard, Chattam
Polson, Andrew
Porter, William
Porter, Mitchell
Porter, John
Portwood, Page
Poston, Richard
Potter, William
Prather, Charles
Prather, Thomas
Preston, Robert
Preston, Walter
Price, James
Price, Jonathan
Price, Thomas
Price John
Price, Samuel
Pruitt, Martin

KING'S MOUNTAIN SOLDIERS

Purviance, James
Purviance, William
Purviance, Richard
Pryor, Mathew

Quarles, Francis
Quarles, John

Rabb, William (k)
Rankin, William
Rankin, David
Rawlings, Asahl (?)
Reagan, Jeremiah (?)
Reamy, Daniel
Reazer, Peter
Reed, John
Reed, Benjamin
Reed, James
Reed, Thomas
Reed, William
Reed, Joseph
Reed, Samuel
Reed, David
Reed, Lovett
Reed, Abraham
Reep, Adam
Reep, Michael (?)
Regan, Charles
Remfeldt, Henry (?)
Reese, James
Reese, David
Reeves, Asher
Reeves, William
Reynolds, Asher
Reynolds, Elisha
Reynolds, Henry
Reynolds, Nathaniel
Rhea, John
Rhea, Joseph
Rice, John
Richardson, Amos
Richardson, James
Riggins, James
Ritchie, Alexander
Ritchie, Samuel
Ritchie, William
Robertson, Joseph
Robertson, William (w)
Robertson, Thomas
Robertson, William
Robertson, John
Roberts, David
Roberts, James
Roberts, Joshua
Roberts, Edward
Robinson, William
Robinson, Thomas
Roddy, James
Rogers, William
Rogers, Benjamin
Roler, James
Roler, Martin
Roper, Roger

Roper, Drury
Ross, John
Ross, Isaac
Rudd, Burlington
Russell, Robert
Russell, Moses
Rutherford, Absolm
Rutherford, William

Sample, Samuel
Sawyers, John
Sarrett, Allen
Scott, Samuel
Scott, Alexander
Scott, Robert
Scott, Joseph
Scott, Joseph Jr.
Scott, Thomas
Scott, Walter
Scott, William
Scott, Samuel Sr.
Scott, John
Scott, Arthur
Scott, James
Self, Thomas
Selman, Jeremiah
Sevier, Joseph
Sevier, James
Sevier, Abraham
Sevier, Joseph II
Sellers, James
Sharp, Benjamin
Sharp, Robert
Sharp, John
Sharp, Samuel
Sharp, Edward
Sharp, James
Sharp, Richard
Sharp, Thomas E.
Sharp, William
Shannon, Thomas
Shaver, Michael
Shaver, Paul
Shaver, Frederick
Shelby, Moses (w)
Shelby, John
Shelby, David
Shelby, Thomas
Sherrill, Samuel Sr.
Sherrill, Adam
Sherrill, George
Sherrill, Samuel Jr.
Shipp, Thomas
Shirley, John
Shote, Thomas
Shook, Greenbury
Singleton, Richard
Simms, James
Simms, John
Siske, Daniel (k)
Siske, Bartlett
Skaggs, John (w)
Skaggs, Henry

Sloan, Alexander
Sloan, William
Sloan, John
Smart, John (k)
Smallwood, William
Smith, David
Smith, Edward
Smith, John
Smith, William
Smith, Henry
Smith, James
Smith, Obediah
Smith, Ransom
Smith, Eaton
Smith, Edward
Smith, George
Smith, Harnett
Smith, Phillip
Smith, Edward
Smith, Leighton
Snodgrass, William
Snodgrass, James
Snoddy, John
Somers, John
Sorter, William
Speltz, John
Stamey, John
Starnes, Nicholas
Steed, Thomas
Steele, William (k)
Steele, John
Steele, Samuel
Steele, Joseph
Steen, James (k)
Stellars, James
Stephens, Jacob
Stephens, Mashack
Stencipher, Joseph
Sterling, Robert
Stevenson, John
Stewart, James
Stewart, William
Stockton, John
Stockton, George
Stockton, William
Stone, William
Stone, Conway
Stone, Ezekial
Stone, Solomon
Stovall, Bartholemew
Stribling, Clayton
Street, Anthony Waddy
Sufferet, John
Sutherland, David
Swadley, Mark
Sweet, Benjamin
Sweeney, Moses
Sword, Michael

KING'S MOUNTAIN SOLDIERS

Tabor, William
Taff, George
Talbert, Charles
Talbot, Mathew Jr.
Talbot, James (?)
Talbot, Thomas (?)
Tate, John
Tate, Robert
Tate, David
Tate, Samuel
Tatum, James
Tatum, Andrew
Taylor, Andrew
Taylor, Andrew Jr.
Taylor, Isaac
Taylor, James
Taylor, James
Taylor, Leroy
Taylor, Parmenus
Temple, Major
Templeton, John
Terrell, Richmond
Terrell, Micajah
Terrell, William
Thatcher, Benjamin
Thomas, John
Thompson, William
Thompson, Alexander
Thompson, John
Thompson, Samuel
Thurman, Phillip
Tillman, Phillip
Tinsley, Golden
Todd, James
Topp, William
Topp, Tom
Tubb, John (w)
Tucker, John
Turnley, George
Turnley, Peter
Trail, James
Trice, James
Turney, Peter (?)
Twitty, William
Twitty, Anthony

Utterly, William

Vance, James
Vance, John
Vance, Samuel

Waddell, Martin
Waddell, John
Waldrin, Peter
Walker, William
Walker, John
Wallace, Thomas

Wallace, John
Walling, William
Walton, William
Walton, Martin
Ward, David
Ward, William
Watkins, George
Watson, David
Watson, Samuel
Watson, William (k)
Weakly, Robert
Wear, John
Weaver, John
Webb, George
Weir, John
Wells, Joseph
Wells, Joseph
Welchel, John
Welchel, Francis
Welchel, David
Welchel, William
Welchel, John
White, William
White, Benjamin
White, Gordon
White, Isaac
Whitesides, John
Whit, Charles
Whitten, Solomon
Wilfong, John (w)
Williams, Benjamin
Williams, James
Williams, Phillip
Williams, Charles
Williams, John
Williams, Shadrack
Williams, Daniel
Williams, Samuel

Williams, Robert
Williams, Mathew
Willis, Smith
Williamson, John
Willoughby, William
Willoughby, Mathew
Williford, Jacob
Wilson, Robert
Wilson, Joseph
Winstead, Francis (?)
Withers, John
Withers, Elisha
Witherspoon, John
Withrow, James
Wood, Obediah
Woods, Michael
Woods, Jonathan
Woods, John
Woolsey, Thomas
Word, Charles (k)
Word, Thomas
Word, Peter
Word, John
Word, Cuthbert
Wynn, William
Wyley, John
Wyley, James
Wyley, Alexander
Yancey, Ambrose
Yates, Samuel (?)
Yeary, Henry
Yontz, George
Young, Robert
Young, Thomas
Young, William
Young, James
Young, Isham (?)
Young, Samuel

Painting by Valosio, depicting Greer as he barged in on Congress to announce the King's Mountain victory. Painting hangs in Tennessee State Museum. Courtesy Tennessee Conservationist.

ADDITIONAL NAMES

OFFICERS

Allison, Robert, Capt.
Buchanan, William, Capt.
Bryan, John, Capt.
Boys, William, Capt.
Chisolm, Elijah, Capt.
Carnes, John, Capt.
Cavett, Moses, Capt.
Christie, Colonel
Donelson, John, Capt.
Evans, Nathaniel, Capt.
Fain, John, Captain
Gibson, James, Capt.
Gillespie, George, Col.
Gambrel, Captain
Harrison, Michael, Capt.
Hicks, William, Capt.
Hoskins, Ninnam, Capt.
Keys, John, Captain
Kyle, Robert, Capt.
Mall, Peter, Capt.
Morgan, Charles, Capt.
McNabb, John, Capt.
Robertson, Elijah
Roddye, James, Capt.
Ridley, George, Capt.
Sherrill, William, Capt.
Shelby, James, Capt.
Smith, Ezekial, Capt.
Stewart, Thomas, Major
Wilfong, George, Major
Warren, Captain

Adair, John
Alexander, William
Arney, Christian
Ayers, Elihu
Burus, David
Billings, Jasper
Brotherton, Thomas
Bryan, Robert
Ballard, Devereau
Barker, Hezekiah
Bickley, William
Brooks, Littleton
Beattie, Joseph
Bolick, Caspar
Bowles, Benjamin
Cavett, Richard
Condry, William
Cooper, James (k)
Cross, William
Cross, Abraham
Callaway, Joseph
Chapman, Joseph
Church, Amos
Cline, Michael
Cole, Jobe
Chandler, Bailey
Dunsmore, James
Denman, John
Dickenson, Isham
Dobson, John
Fry, Phillip
Ferguson, Joseph
Foster, Anthony

Gabriel, James
Gilbreath, Alexander
Goodlett, William
Gregory, William
Henry, David
Haas, John
Haas, Simon
Hahn, Joshua
Hahn, Benedict
Hammons, Benjamin
Hammons, John
Harris, William
Hofner, Nicholas
Hunt, Abraham
Hunt, John
Hardmark, Charles
Johnson, George Sr.
Johnson, William
King, Thomas
Keeton, Hezekiah
Kuykendall, Simon
Leeper, Mathew
Laws, David
Lutz, Jacob
Mitchell, David
Montgomery, John
Morgan, Benjamin
Proffit, Pleasant
Parks, John
Powell, William
Simms, Littlepage
Simpson, William
Stevenson, James

Setzer, John
Shell, Michael
Sherrill, Uriah
Sigmon, Palsor
Simpson, William
Rose, Sterling
Rumfeld, Henry
Scurlock, James
Schultz, Martin
Smith, Jones
Smool, James
Sparks, John
Spicer, William
Stamper, Joel
Summerlin, William
Swanson, John
Smithers, Gabriel
Starnes, Peter
Toliver, Jesse
Toliver, Moses
Treadway, Robert
Tippong, Conrad
Turbyfill, John
Vickers, Elijah
Weaver, Frederick
Wall, Jacob
Wilson, Andrew
Wilson, John
Waters, Moses
Whitaker, John
Whitner, Abraham
Whitner, Daniel
White, Solomon
Yoder, Conrad

Pemberton Oak: Colonel John Pemberton mustered his men under this oak in 1780 enroute to King's Mountain. Oak still stands and Pemberton descendants still own the property. Soldiers of five wars have camped under this tree.

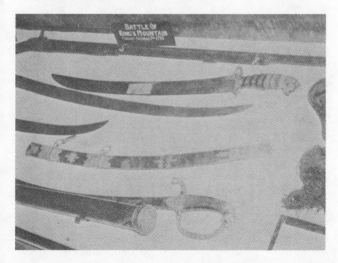

Robert Young gun; Ferguson sword, field glasses and sash, Tennessee State Museum, Nashville.

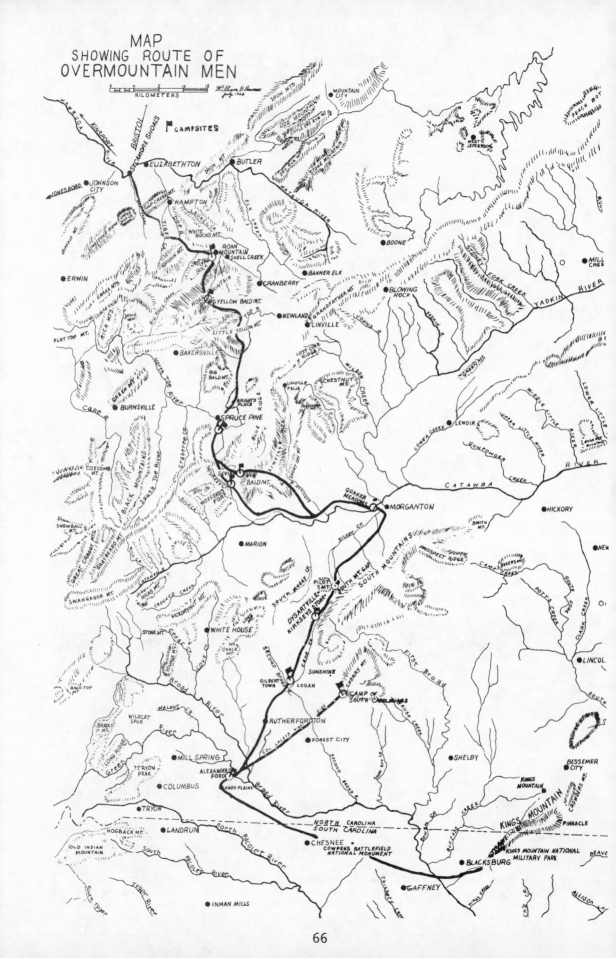

MAP
SHOWING ROUTE OF
OVERMOUNTAIN MEN

William D. Bowman
July 1968

KILOMETERS

FROM KING'S MOUNTAIN TO PARIS PEACE TREATY

The King's Mountain victory was an important link in the chain of events that brought the British to the Paris Peace Table. During the rough winter of 1780-1781, General Washington's army of 3,500 men were encamped outside New York. Heavy snows, little food, no pay or clothing gave poor incentive for the dispirited army to attack a well-fed British force of over 10,000, housed comfortably in the New York Barracks. The salvation of Washington's force was the concentrated effort being undertaken by Cornwallis in the South. This took the pressure off the northern army.

The treason of Benedict Arnold cast a curtain of gloom over the cause of Liberty. General Washington was greatly upset over this betrayal by one of his officers. American affairs and hopes looked anything but bright as the year 1781 dawned. Continental money was worthless and troop mutinies were commonplace. The two men responsible for changing the course of events were Robert Morris and John Laurens. Morris managed to raise money to aid Washington in supplying his men, and John Laurens was sent to seek more aid from France. The slowness of the French Ministry, in responding to America's request for help, irked young Laurens. He managed to obtain an interview with the French King, who agreed to supply desperately needed backing. Without the aid secured by these men, General Washington could not have continued the war effort. News that the French Fleet was sailing to American waters, and other promised help, charged the air with new hope. Fresh plans and actions were contemplated and enlistments increased.

John Laurens was 28 years old when Congress sent him to France in an effort to secure money in 1780. Young Laurens served with Washington from Brandywine to York Town; was killed in a South Carolina skirmish, August 27, 1782.

General William Lee Davidson experienced the desperate winter of 1777-78 at Valley Forge. Davidson County, North Carolina and Davidson College were named in his honor.

Robert Morris raised money with his own private credit, on several occasions, to aid General Washington in clothing and feeding the American Army. Final victory would have been impossible without his help. Morris served time in a debtor's prison, after the war, because of financial failures.

Shortly after the King's Mountain Battle, General William Lee Davidson and Captain W. R. Davie began to assemble a force in New Providence. They had hopes of raising a formidable army with which to confront Cornwallis. Because of the inactivity in the North, General Washington had sent Generals Daniel Morgan and Smallwood, with a detachment of Maryland recruits, to aid in the southern cause. General Gates had been able to assemble about 1,200 men from his defeated Camden army. General Stephens was sent to North Carolina with a force of newly enlisted Virginia Militia.

General Davidson, in charge of the Salisbury District, thought the time and conditions were right to organize a strong campaign. Messages were sent across the mountains, seeking assistance from the Overmountain riflemen. In response, Colonel John Sevier called a meeting of his officers at Jonesborough, November 20, 1780, to discuss the situation. Captains James Stinson, James Gibson and Luke Bower were directed to cross the mountains with 130 men to join Davidson. A similar request had been sent to Colonel Isaac Shelby, but he was already with General Morgan in an advisory capacity. This projected campaign was cancelled before it actually started.

Congress, having lost faith in Gates, asked General Washington to appoint a replacement. Washington's choice was Major-General Nathaniel Greene. General Greene had recently resigned his position as Quartermaster-General of the Continental Army. Congress, tired of the big commissions made by quartermasters, had placed them all on salary. This move caused much resentment and created problems in the supply department. Greene, not liking the situation, resigned and thus became available for active duty in the field. He

proved a good commander during the last years of the war. No great victories are recorded to his credit, but his type of warfare proved destructive to the British strength. Greene would often say after a battle, "We fight, get beaten and fight again."

General Greene arrived in Charlotte, North Carolina, December 1780, and with a very brief ceremony assumed the command of the southern branch of the Continental Army. This was to herald a year of much bloodshed in the Carolinas, Georgia and Virginia, the final battlefields of the Revolutionary War.

General Greene takes over the southern command from General Gates at Charlotte, North Carolina. King's Mountain National Military Park.

Partisan conflicts, between the Tories and Whigs, were continuing in many southern sections. We cite one such incident that took place on the Yadkin River eight days after the King's Mountain victory. A company of 300 Surry County Tories had been recruited to join the Loyalist cause. They had enlisted under Colonel Gideon Wright and his brother Captain Hezikiah Wright. They probably had not learned of the King's Mountain Battle, as they were marching to join General Cornwallis at Charlotte. They plundered, killed and burned on their march toward the British force. Colonel Joseph Williams, living near Shallow Ford on the Yadkin, called together some 200 riflemen from the area. They set up an ambush at the ford and awaited the Tory party. The 300 loyalists prepared to cross the river, not suspecting any opposition. The conflict was short, hard and decisive. The Tories, badly beaten, fled and scattered.

Now, back to the Overmountain men on the frontier, September 1780. They were preparing for the mountain crossing to meet Colonel Ferguson. When the British agents learned that this big force of riflemen would be absent from the settlements, they planned to use this opportunity to their advantage. They told the Cherokee Chiefs that only young boys and old men would be left to defend the settlements. Now was the time to attack, when they were weak. Pack horse loads of supplies were brought in from the Augusta depot. War councils were under way in most of the towns.

The old chiefs of the Overhill towns tried to dissuade the younger chiefs from this course of action, but their voices were not heeded. Attakullakulla, known as "The Little Carpenter," died during 1780. His son, Dragging Canoe, did not agree with his diplomatic father in treating with the whites. Attakullakulla had been the controlling spirit in the political and peace keeping councils of the Cherokee. Now he was gone. Oconostota, War Chief of many years, was getting old and his words were not heard. The disregard of Indian rights by many white settlers, in building cabins on Indian land, gave the English agents receptive ears among the young resentful warriors. The atmosphere was right for an all out war on the white settlements.

Attakullakulla, Cherokee Peace Chief often called "The Little Carpenter."

Oconostota resigned as War Chief in 1782. The Chota Treaty with Sevier that year was his last public appearance at a White-Indian council. Old and nearly blind, Oconostota, along with Nancy Ward and other members of the family, spent the winter of 1782-83 in the home of Joseph Martin on Long Island (Kingsport). In the spring, feeling the end near, he asked Martin to take him back to his beloved Chota. Oconostota was buried with Christian rites in a canoe coffin.

BOYD'S CREEK BATTLE

Major Joseph Martin, Virginia's Agent to the Cherokees, had been in the Overhill towns in an attempt to restrain the Indians from going on the warpath. He was unsuccessful in his mission. John McDonald, British Agent, tried to imprison Martin; but Chiefs Oconostota and Hanging Maw had sufficient influence to prevent this act. The Agents were able to persuade the younger chiefs to take Dragging Canoe by the arm and join in the war against the settlers. The Indians, unable to obtain supplies from the Americans, had turned to the British. The English agents used the Augusta depot to their advantage. They told the chiefs that any Indian towns that stayed friendly and peaceful toward the Americans would get no supplies. The Indians were urged to speed their war preparations; and a large force of several hundred warriors was assembled. This new alliance, with the British, was to prove a disastrous move for the Cherokee.

Nancy Ward, friend of the white and red people, operated an Inn on Womankiller Ford of the Ocoee River near Benton, Tennessee. Died 1824.

Nancy Ward again moved to befriend the whites. This Cherokee Chieftainess, anxious to save her people from utter destruction, was trying to carry on the role of her Uncle Attakullakulla in smoothing over the difficulties that were constantly arising. Knowing that she could not stop the warriors from taking the warpath, she sent warning of the impending attacks by Isaac Thomas, Ellis Hardin and William Springstone. These white traders slipped out of the Indian towns and carried word to the white settlements.

Many people have tried to call Nancy Ward a traitor to her people. Nothing is further from the truth. She realized that the Indians were unable to cope with the white man's superior know-how, strength and numbers. She struggled desperately to save her people from the very tragedy that finally came to their homes, towns and nation. Nancy Ward was held in respect by the red people and the white settlers. Her constant expression had been, *"The white men are our brothers; the same house shelters us, the same sky covers us all."*

Isaac Thomas and Ellis Hardin delivered the warning to the Nolichucky and Watauga people. William Springstone went on to Virginia and delivered a like message to Colonel Arthur Campbell. Campbell and Joseph Martin called a meeting of the officials and militia heads at Martin's Trading Post on Long Island (Kingsport). It was decided that a request to General Davidson, for a Commanding Officer, would make the campaign official. While all this was taking place, the Indians were raiding exposed cabins.

Colonel John Sevier, busy with other problems and troop requests from General Davidson, did not attend the Long Island meeting. He had been expecting this Indian attack, even before leaving for the King's Mountain campaign. He had dispatched Captain George Russell and his company, soon after the battle, on a forced march home in case hostile Indians approached the Nolichucky settlements.

Sevier, receiving the warning from Nancy Ward of the impending attack, moved immediately to raise a force to confront the invaders. Sevier believed that offense was the best defense. His riders called the men to muster at once, as the exposed Nolichucky frontier could not wait for the long drawn-out planning of the Martin-Campbell campaign. It is assumed that he sent word of his action.

The rendezvous was set at Swann Pond on Lick Creek in Greene County, December 15, 1780. Leading 200 men, Sevier started toward Indian territory. The second night out they camped on Long Island of the Nolichucky River. Captain Gist, on a scouting tour, sighted one party of warriors. Firing from horseback, the party returned to camp without attempting to fight the Indians. Sevier prepared for a possible night attack by placing his men in battle arrangement. After stationing guards in all quarters, the men slept on their arms. During the night Captain Pruett arrived with his men, and by daybreak other companies had caught up with the main force.

Early next morning Colonel Sevier pushed across the French Broad River at Big Island Ford. His force now numbered 300 men. As the riflemen moved nearer the Overhill country, signs indicated that a large force lay ahead; but Sevier led his men deeper into the Indian territory. The third night they camped near Boyd's Creek in the present Sevier County. Before daybreak next morning, Captain Stinson, in charge of the scouting patrol, discovered the main Indian camp about three miles from that of the white force. The

Braves, hoping to draw Sevier's force into an ambush, had left their campfires burning. Colonel Sevier seldom rushed into a situation until he looked it over. His acquaintance with the red man's tactics had saved him many times. Catching up to his advance scouts, he carefully studied the landscape in an effort to locate the positions of the large bands of warriors. He soon discovered the Indians arranged in a half-moon shape, ready to pounce on the pioneer riflemen should they charge the blazing campfires.

The following description of the battle is taken from Ramsey's **Annals of Tennessee**.

Clarke-Martin Fight

A reinforcement was immediately ordered to the front, and the guard was directed, if it came up with the Indians, to fire upon them and retreat, and thus draw them on. Three quarters of a mile from their camp, the enemy fired upon the advance guard from their ambuscade. The whites returned the fire and retreated, and, as had been anticipated, was pursued by the enemy till it joined the main body. This was formed into three divisions; the center commanded by Colonel Sevier, the right wing by Major Walton, and the left by Major Jonathan Tipton. Orders were given that as soon as the enemy should approach the front, the right wing should wheel to the left, and the left wing to the right, and thus enclose them. In this order were the troops arranged when they met the Indians at Cedar Springs, who rushed forward after the guard with great rapidity, till checked by the opposition of the main body. Major Walton with the right wing wheeled briskly to the left, and performed the order which he was to execute with precise accuracy. But the left wing moved to the right with less celerity, and when the center fired upon the Indians, doing immense execution, the latter retreated through the unoccupied space left open between the extremes of the right and left wings, and running into a swamp escaped the destruction which otherwise seemed ready to involve them. The victory was decisive. The loss of the enemy amounted to twenty-eight killed on the ground and very many wounded, who got off without being taken. On the side of Sevier's troops not a man was wounded. The victorious little army then returned to Big Island and waited there for the arrival of the reinforcements that promised to follow.

The Indians had not expected to meet this large well-organized force. They had been led to believe that all the fighting men were across the mountain battling Ferguson. They had also been told, by these agents, that the well-trained British forces would soon defeat the untrained backwoodsmen. Their plans to retake their land by running the settlers back across the mountains had again gone amiss.

Quoting another descriptive narrative from Ramsey: *The Indians had formed in a half moon, and lay concealed in the grass. Had their stratagem not been discovered, their position and shape of the ground, would have enabled them to enclose and overcome the horsemen. Lieutenant Lane and John Ward had dismounted for the fight, when Sevier, having noticed the semicircular position of the Indians, ordered a halt, with the purpose of engaging the top extremes of the Indian line, and keeping up the action until the other part of his troops could come up. Lane and his comrade, Ward, remounted and fell back upon Sevier without being hurt, though fired at by several warriors near them. A brief fire was, for a short time, kept up by Sevier's party and the nearest Indians. The troops behind, hearing the first fire, had quickened their pace and were coming in sight. James Roddy, with about twenty men, quickly came up, and soon after the main body of the troops. The Indians*

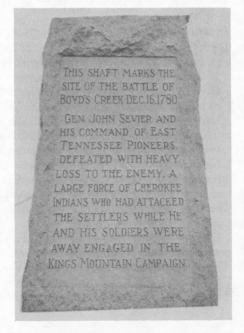

THIS SHAFT MARKS THE SITE OF THE BATTLE OF BOYD'S CREEK DEC. 16, 1780

GEN. JOHN SEVIER AND HIS COMMAND OF EAST TENNESSEE PIONEERS DEFEATED WITH HEAVY LOSS TO THE ENEMY, A LARGE FORCE OF CHEROKEE INDIANS WHO HAD ATTACKED THE SETTLERS WHILE HE AND HIS SOLDIERS WERE AWAY ENGAGED IN THE KINGS MOUNTAIN CAMPAIGN

noticed the reinforcements and closed their lines. Sevier immediately ordered the charge, which would have been still more fatal, but that the pursuit led through a swampy branch, which impeded the progress of the horsemen.

In the charge Sevier was in close pursuit of a warrior, who finding that he would be overtaken, turned and fired at him. The bullet cut the hair of his temple without doing further injury. Sevier then spurred his horse forward and attempted to kill the Indian with his sword, having emptied his pistols in the first moments of the charge. The warrior parried the licks from the sword with his empty gun. The conflict was becoming doubtful between the combatants thus engaged, when one of the soldiers, rather ungallantly, came up, shot the warrior, and decided the combat in favor of his Commander.

The horse of Adam Sherrill (John Sevier's brother-in-law) threw his rider, and in the fall some of his ribs were broken. An Indian sprang upon him with his tomahawk drawn. When in the act of striking, a ball from a comrade's rifle brought him to the ground, and Sherrill escaped. After a short pursuit, the Indians dispersed into the adjoining highlands and knolls, where the calvary could not pursue them. Of the whites not one was killed but three seriously wounded.

The Boyd's Creek battle is one of the few Indian fights, led by Colonel John Sevier, of which we have a detailed description. This was the first offensive campaign in which he was in command. All told, during his career, Sevier fought thirty-five Indian battles and never lost one. Very few of his men were killed or wounded. He is ranked first, by many writers, of all the Indian fighters. The red men feared and respected him. He led his men rather than sending them into battle.

Ramsey lists the following officers as participating in the Boyd's Creek Battle: Landon Carter, James Sevier, Abraham Sevier, Thomas Gist, Abel Pearson, James Hubbard, Ben Sharpe, Samuel Hadley, Jacob Brown, Jeremiah Jack, Nathan Gaun, Isaac Taylor, George Doherty, and George Russell. There were other officers not listed.

After the battle, Sevier and his men pulled back to Big Island to wait the arrival of Colonel Arthur Campbell.

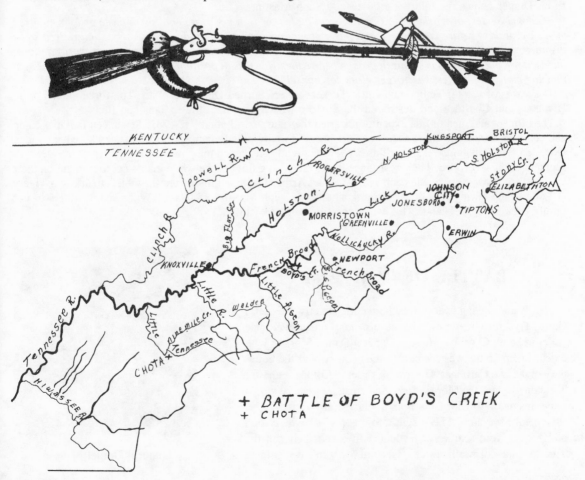

+ BATTLE OF BOYD'S CREEK
+ CHOTA

A messenger from Campbell stated that he would be there within the week, and requested Sevier to delay advancing on the Indian towns until the forces were joined. Campbell did not arrive on schedule. Game was scarce on the Island, and Sevier decided to move back to the Boyd's Creek area. Seasoned hunters, like Isaac Thomas and William Bean, were unable to find food. The men had to rely on parched acorns, corn, nuts and haws. A stray cow and calf found in the woods helped. This campsite was known for many years as "Hungry Camp." The stay here was short, as Colonel Arthur Campbell, with his Virginia Regiment, and Major Joseph Martin, with the Sullivan riflemen, soon joined the Sevier force. The troops now numbered about 700 mounted men. Colonel Arthur Campbell shared his limited food supply with Sevier's men.

On December 23rd, they marched to the Tennessee River. Scouts reported that the main crossing at Maliquo was heavily guarded. The Pioneer force moved upstream opposite Tommotley and forded the Tennessee River at this point December 24th. This maneuver upset the Indian plan of attack.

The march was continued to Chota, arriving there December 25th. Large bodies of Indian warriors were seen along the hills overlooking the route of march. The large body of riflemen discouraged any attack. A few scattered shots were exchanged between the two forces. Camp was made near Chota. Sentries and guards were posted in every direction. Food to feed the hungry men was obtained from the Indians. Nancy Ward sent a small herd of cattle to the white soldier's camp. Much of Christmas night was spent cooking and eating the fresh meat.

Colonel Elijah Clarke, who had accompanied Sevier with his Georgia riflemen, had a fight with Major Martin over the meat. Colonel Clarke, seeing the cattle being driven into camp, ordered his men to kill and dress the beef. Major Martin, who had married Betsy the daughter of Nancy Ward, felt that he was responsible for the gift. He resented Clarke taking over without his consent. Martin and a company of his men forcibly took the dressed and quartered beefs, hanging from tree limbs. When Colonel Clarke returned and learned what had happened, he confronted Martin. Angry words were exchanged between the two six-foot stalwarts. A man to man fight ensued.

Joseph Martin and Arthur Campbell were resentful because of Sevier's early march and victory at Boyd's Creek. Angry words were spoken and a rift, between the Sullivan and Washington County men, was opened. From Draper comes the following quote of Joseph Martin.

"Colonel Sevier, of Washington County, went on his own, in his own behalf with three or four hundred men several days before the army, met a party of Indians, had a little fight, killed a few, and retired some distance, waiting for the main army. This was complained of at the time not only as an unauthorized move, but as apprizing the Indians of our approach before the army was in position to act efficiently. It was thought that the motive of Sevier was to get glory for himself."

The towns of Chota, Tellico and Little Tuskegee were burned December 28th. The force moved on to Hiwassee and Chestuee and destroyed these two towns from which the Indians had fled.

The officers and men of this expedition started the return trip January 1, 1781. Seventeen Indian women and children were taken along as hostage prisoners. Twenty-nine Indian warriors had been killed and many wounded. The damaging results of this expedition greatly weakened the power and the spirit of the Overhill segment of the Cherokee. Their resistance to the increasing flow of the white man's encroachment on their lands was to grow more feeble each year. Colonel Arthur Campbell instructed the Chiefs to attend a Treaty at Long Island during July of the coming summer. Joseph Martin took Nancy Ward and members of her family. back to Long Island. This was done for their protection.

BATTLE OF COWPENS

General Daniel Morgan

Shortly after taking over the southern command from General Gates, General Greene established his camp on the Pee Dee River in South Carolina. He sent General Daniel Morgan with a detachment to the western part of the country near the boundary of the two Carolinas. Cornwallis ordered Colonel Banastre Tarleton to attack the Morgan force and crush it, while he would move his army to Morgan's rear to cut off any retreat.

General Morgan had been sent into this region, where food and forage were scarce, and situated in a spot between the Tarleton and Cornwallis forces. General Morgan's detachment numbered about 900 men, including experienced militia and a company of cavalry under Colonel William Washington. Colonel Tarleton commanded a force of 1200 men including his own corps of cavalry. General Morgan had made camp near Cowpens, about five miles south of the North Carolina border. This was the site where the mountaineer army had made a conjunction with the South Carolinians enroute to King's Mountain three months earlier.

Before dawn, January 17th, Morgan had his men fed before arranging them in their battle positions. There was little underbrush in the terrain he selected for the engagement. His main lines were posted on a small ridge between two brooks. His best-trained soldiers were located in the center, the Virginia riflemen on the right and left wings. Colonel Washington and his cavalry unit were located in the rear as reserves. Pickens was in a skirmish position up front, with volunteer riflemen posted on each side of the expected route of Tarleton's approach.

Colonel Banastre Tarleton, British Officer, served with Cornwallis in the Southern Campaign.

Colonel Tarleton moved forward to the attack about eight o'clock in the morning. Two regiments, one regular and the other artillery, were lined up in front. Tarleton brought up the rear with his Cavalry Legion. The initial attack was met with a strong fire from Pickens' men flanking each side. These men retired a short distance, formed lines and fired again. Soon the riflemen posted on the wings were in range and opened fire. These expert marksmen were taking a heavy toll on the British and caused the front lines to give way. They began to retreat when Morgan's militia charged with bayonets. Both wings moved forward as the bayonet charge caused the Tory line to break and run. The Loyalists threw down their guns and everything else that hindered their running. Tarleton was never able to check their chaotic, scared flight. By this time Washington's cavalry charged Tarleton's Dragoons. They also broke and fled. The pursuit was continued for 20 miles before the American units were ordered back. It was a complete victory for the Patriots.

British losses in the battle were 300 or more killed and wounded, over 500 privates taken as prisoners, 29 officers captured. In addition, 800 guns, 100 horses, 35 wagons and two field pieces were taken. The cumbersome wagons and other baggage were destroyed. General Morgan knew that General Cornwallis would move fast, in an effort to cut him off and free the prisoners. He did not want to be burdened with the baggage and wagons.

The American losses were 12 killed and 60 wounded. Taking his wounded and forming his prisoners into a line of march, General Morgan moved into North Carolina and set his course toward the Virginia border. Heavy rains filled the streams and made progress slow. Parties of Tories caught up to the rear, and every creek and river crossing had to be defended. The large body of prisoners caused the march to move slower than it would ordinarily. It was at Cowan's Ford on the Catawba River that General Davidson, in charge of a rear guard action, was killed by Tories. General Greene had left his command and joined Morgan to aid in this great escape with 500 prisoners. Cornwallis nearly caught the Morgan force on one or two occasions, but high water delayed him, especially at the Yadkin. He pursued the Americans to the Dan River where he turned back. Generals Greene and Morgan continued on into Virginia.

Generals Greene and Morgan took time to rest their united forces, dispose of their prisoners and recruit more men. One of the requests for help went to the Overmountain leaders, Colonels Shelby and Sevier. Colonel Sevier, busy planning a campaign against the Middle Towns of the Cherokee, delegated Major Charles Robertson to lead a battalion to Greene's assistance. Robertson chose three Captains and their companies, numbering about 130 men. They left on the long march across the mountains the latter part of February, 1781. They reached Greene's Camp, near the site of the battle of Alamance, March 6th. Colonel Shelby did not lead a detachment to join Greene at this time. Colonel William Campbell arrived from Virginia with 60 men. Major Robertson's men were placed under Campbell's command.

GUILFORD COURTHOUSE BATTLE

General Cornwallis had issued a call to the Tories of North Carolina to join the King's cause. The response was not very satisfactory. General Pickens and his men were inflicting such heavy losses on Tory groups assembling to join Cornwallis, that this had a discouraging effect on others. Colonel Tarleton, the supporting arm of General Cornwallis, did not measure up to his vaulted reputation after King's Mountain and Cowpens. On several occasions he flinched at meeting the Patriots on equal terms.

General Greene avoided a direct encounter with Cornwallis until he felt that his force was in favorable number to match the British. Another blow to Greene was losing General Morgan. Cowpens was the last battle for this valiant General. Troubled with rheumatism and fever, he was unable to continue active duty.

The Americans moved into position sometime during the day of March 14th. Cornwallis learned this the same day, so early morning, March 15th, he marched his forces toward Greene's position. This was an encounter that the British General had been trying to maneuver Greene into making for several weeks.

General Greene's force was larger in number than the British, but his Militia were inexperienced fighters and had very little military training. The first line of the Patriot defense was made up of raw recruits of the North Carolina Militia. The Virginia Militia, almost as inexperienced,

Major-General Nathaniel Greene, American Commander in the South during 1780-1781.

Americans withdrawing from battlefield after Guilford Courthouse Battle. Guilford Courthouse National Military Park.

formed the second line. Continental troops made up the third line. Colonel Henry Lee and Colonel William Campbell's riflemen formed on the left wing, and Colonel William Washington, with cavalry and other continental troops, were placed on the right flank.

The British force was well organized, experienced and disciplined. It was a bloody battle. The first line of the Americans broke at the first attack. The second line held for a while, but they also broke and fell back. The right and left wings had become engaged in separate fights, almost removed from the main battle. The riflemen on both wings were causing the British heavy losses; but in spite of this, the Loyalists had reached a position from which they could hit the American positions with grape and canister. General Greene, not knowing that he held the advantage, was unwilling to risk his men in a final, desperate and costly charge. Wanting to save his force for other battles, he sounded orders to retreat. Thus, General Cornwallis gained the field of battle but his heavy loss made it a doubtful victory. The British loss, after the two and one-half hour bloody struggle, was over 600 casualties.

The Guilford Courthouse Battle climaxed a winter campaign that was very damaging to the British cause: the King's Mountain catastrophe, the defeat at Cowpens and now the Guilford debacle. Actually, for the British, all reports indicate that it was one of the severest engagements of the southern campaign.

General Cornwallis left the field of battle almost immediately and marched toward the seacoast, to be nearer his source of supply. He stopped at Cross Creek (Fayetteville, North Carolina), thinking this Tory country a safe haven but was disappointed in two ways. The Scots settled in the area did not flock to join the British force. Another reason why the British Commander did not stop long was that he was too far from a good port. Ships and boats could not navigate the Cape Fear River to bring supplies. The British were in great need of medical, camping and food sources. Headquarters was established in Wilmington.

General Greene had followed the British, hoping to force another encounter; but Cornwallis, unwilling to risk another engagement until better prepared, destroyed bridges, slowing Greene's efforts to catch up with the main force. General Greene changed his direction and marched into South Carolina to his former camp on Pee Dee River.

The Tory-infested country of North Carolina, between the Yadkin River and the Cape Fear, broke into a turmoil that was to leave communities torn asunder for several generations. Under the umbrella of the Cornwallis army they plundered, robbed, killed, burned and harassed Whig homes. David "Scaldhead" Fanning was one of the worst of the Tory leaders. He seemed to have a fatal attraction and quality that enlisted bloodthirsty men to his small army. They raided and killed in the name of the Crown but somehow evaded the regular British-American battles. Raiding courts was one of Fanning's special accomplishments. On one occasion they captured the Court of Chatham County at Pittsboro, and later raided the Hillsborough Court where they captured Governor Thomas Burke and other prominent Whigs. These prisoners were taken to Wilmington, North Carolina, and thrown into Major Craig's bull-pen prison. The Whigs, on the other hand, were equally cruel in their reprisal on Tory families.

Another hated Tory leader was Bloody Bill Cunningham. He had no regard for promises made or guarantees of safe conduct to surrendered prisoners. On many occasions Cunningham promised Whigs that they would be granted life and freedom, if they would throw down their arms and march out the doors of their fortification with their arms raised. As soon as they were outside, Bloody Bill's men would murder them in cold blood.

GREASY COVE MUSTER

In February, 1781, Governor Abner Nash commissioned John Sevier as a full Colonel, replacing Colonel John Carter who died during 1780. Before news of the appointment reached the West, Sevier was off on another Indian campaign. Some of the raids on the Nolichucky Settlements were blamed on the Middle Towns of the Cherokee Nation, located in the Western North Carolina area. Colonel Sevier had summoned his men to muster in Greasy Cove (Unicoi County, Tennessee) early March, 1781. Three companies, commanded by Captains Valentine Sevier, James Stinson, and David McNabb, assembled. Jonathan Tipton served as Major during this expedition.

They crossed Red Bank Ford off the Nolichucky River, followed the trail through Coxe's Cove Gap (now known as Spivey's Gap), rode on to Cane River which they followed some distance, crossed to Ivey Creek and continued on to an old Indian warpath which they followed to the Tuckasegee River. They made a surprise attack on the town of Tuckasegee, killing 50 or more warriors. Several women and children were taken as hostages. More than twelve Indian Towns were destroyed. The return march of Sevier's force was made through Indian Gap of the Smoky Mountains, down to the crossing of French Broad near the present

Rendering Bear Grease in Greasy Cove from a painting by Edyth Price.

town of Newport and on home. Two casualties were suffered on this trip.

During an attack on Cowee, Nathaniel Davis was seriously wounded and John Bond killed. Sevier sent Davis, accompanied by a member of the force, back home by way of the trail they had traveled going down. Nathaniel Davis did not reach home, as he died in Greasy Cove and was buried there.

An earlier plan to send a force against the Middle Towns had been attempted during August, 1780. About 100 men mustered in Greasy Cove near Red Bank Ford on the Nolichucky River. A small skirmish at the ford, the shooting at one of the troop out hunting and the finding of a dead Indian, discouraged the undertaking. They feared that raiding parties were in the area and would use their absence as a good opportunity to attack their settlements. The men returned to their homes.

Red Bank Ford on the Nolichucky River, where crossings were made before bridge was built (Near Erwin, Tennessee).

YORK TOWN

General Cornwallis remained in Wilmington long enough to reorganize his army, replenish his supplies and restore the morale of his men. As he speculated on the progress of the war, he returned to the premise that Virginia was the key to overcoming the southern states. Ignoring General Clinton's advice, he marched toward Virginia the last of April or the first of May. There was friction between the two Generals. Cornwallis aspired to the Commander-in-Chief position held by Clinton. The British force reached Petersburg, Virginia, May 20, 1781. Here junction was made with Generals William Phillips and Benedict Arnold, both commanding sizeable forces.

Benedict Arnold's first exploit, after assuming a British Command, was the burning and plundering of Richmond. Cornwallis did not want the traitor Arnold in his command, so he instructed him to join Clinton in New York. Clinton, likewise reluctant to have him near, sent Arnold to a command in his home state, Connecticut.

General Greene had ordered General Lafayette, with his 3500 men, to remain in Virginia. General Washington meanwhile had

General Benjamin Lincoln surrendered his sword to Cornwallis at Charleston, South Carolina. The Cornwallis sword was surrendered to Lincoln at York Town.

sent General Anthony Wayne to assist Lafayette in the Virginia operation. Both sides moved and countermoved without any significant confrontation. Actions at Hot Water Plantation and Green Springs were the two outstanding engagements preceding York Town.

Clinton had ordered Cornwallis to secure a base for the English Fleet. This was done. Meanwhile, instead of attacking Clinton in New York, General Washington decided to make a campaign against Cornwallis in Virginia. Assembling all the forces, including those of Count Rochambeau, General Von Steuben, General Lincoln, General Henry Knox, Colonel Stephen Moylan, General Lafayette, General Wayne, Duke de Lauzun, Colonel d'Aboville, Colonel Desandrouins and Colonel Querenet, Washington surrounded York Town. Count DeGrasse, Admiral of the French Fleet, blockaded the British on the waterside. The combined American forces numbered about 16,000. Closer and closer Washington's forces drew their lines around the Cornwallis fortifications. They battered with cannon and took the redoubts by assault. With no avenue left for escape, General Cornwallis surrendered October 19, 1781. This was the climatic battle of the Revolutionary War. Nevertheless, hostilities continued for more than a year in several areas of the country.

After the Guilford Courthouse Battle, General Greene followed Cornwallis as far as Ramsey's Mill near the junction of Haw and Deep River. Finding this pursuit impracticable, Greene turned toward South Carolina with plans to attack Lord Rawdon at Camden. Rawdon surprised the Greene forces at Hobkirk's and defeated the Americans, April 25th. The loss on each side has been estimated at 300. General Francis Marion captured a British post at Santee, just a short while before the conflict on Hobkirk Hill. This made Camden an untenable post, so Rawdon pulled out May 10th. About the same time, General Sumpter defeated a British post at Orangeburg and Marion captured Fort Motte. This left the two strongholds of Augusta and Ninety-Six as the only strong points outside Charleston.

Many of the Overmountain men had volunteered to go with Colonel Elijah Clarke into Georgia. They left Colonel Sevier's force after the final phases of the Cherokee Indian Campaign, January 1781. Clarke, his Georgians and the Overmountain men arrived in Georgia in time to assist in clearing the British from that state. They participated

American Battery No. 2 at National Military Park, York Town, Virginia. York Town National Military Park.

Fort Ninety-Six: Picture shows some of the breastworks of the English stronghold in South Carolina. King's Mountain National Military Park.

Night watchman in Philadelphia conducted express rider sent by Washington, with news of the York Town Victory, to door of the President of Congress. Thus, the Government officials learned of the defeat of Cornwallis. The German night watchman continued his rounds crying, "Three o'clock and Cornwallis is taken."

in the recapture of Augusta and most likely took part in the battles of Long Cane and Beattie's Mill.

General Greene attempted to take Ninety-Six during May, but the well-fortified fort withstood the siege. The Americans were unable to breech the outer walls. The report that Rawdon was coming to its relief rushed Greene's final attempt, which also proved fruitless. He pulled his force back further north. It is ironic that the position was evacuated not long after Greene's departure.

Lord Rawdon, unable to maintain the fortified posts covering his supply lines, pulled his various regiments into Charleston. Fugitive Tory families cluttered his march and hampered his campaign tactics. Arriving in Charleston, he boarded a ship, intending to return to England. This vessel was captured by the French and Rawdon was made a prisoner. He left behind a stained career and a dishonorable reputation.

LONG ISLAND TREATY

General Greene appealed to the Overmountain men for help. At the time they received this message, they were in the midst of a Treaty with the Cherokee at Long Island. Colonels Shelby and Sevier were both attending the Council with the Indians. The Treaty-Meet had been scheduled for July 20, 1781 but was a week late in getting started. General Greene had appointed a Commission composed of William Christian, William Preston, Arthur Campbell, Joseph Martin, Robert Sevier (Greene did not know of his death), Evan Shelby, Joseph Williams and John Sevier. This commission was empowered to work out peace agreements with the Cherokee and arrange for an exchange of prisoners.

During the meet, The Tassel, principal speaker for the Cherokee, addressed these remarks to Colonel Sevier. *"I know that you are a man and a warrior. I have heard different talks by different people quite different from what I expected. I fear you must have been angry and that it was caused by some evil persons.....You have risen up from a warrior to be a Beloved Man. I hope your speech will be good."* Colonel Sevier in replying to The Tassel said, *"I have never hated the Cherokee, but have had to fight them for the safety of my people."*

Nancy Ward, Chieftainess of the Cherokee Nation, arose at this point and made a talk. *"You know that women are always looked upon as nothing; but we are your mothers; and you are our sons. Our cry is all for peace; let it continue. This peace must last forever. Let your women's sons be ours; our sons be yours. Let your women hear our words."*

The words moved the assembled group. Nancy Ward's friendship for the whites and her constant efforts to keep peace between the two races had their effect. Colonel William Christian made the reply.

"Mothers: we have listened well to your talk; it is humane...No man can hear it without being moved by it. Such words and thoughts show the world that human nature is the same everywhere. Our women shall hear your words, and we know how they will feel and think of them. We all are descendants of the same women. We will not quarrel with you, because you are our mothers. We will not meddle with your people if they will be still and quiet at home and let us live in peace." (These quotes and records have been taken from Williams' **Tennessee During The Revolution**). This is one of the very few Treaties where no request was made, by the whites, for more Indian land. Nancy Ward has often been characterized as the "Pocahontas of the West." She was no ordinary woman.

During September General Greene made a push against Colonel Stuart, encamped at Eutaw Springs. The British were driven from the field with considerable loss. Much plunder was taken, including an abundance of food. For a period the Americans were able to eat well. The Stuart force moved back to Charleston, leaving that area to the Patriots.

OVERMOUNTAIN MEN VOLUNTEER

More letters and requests from Greene induced Colonels Shelby and Sevier to enlist a force and go to Greene's assistance. The Overmountain men were promised that this enlistment would be for sixty days only. Shelby raised 400; but Sevier, because of the Chickamauga raids, was unwilling to take more than 200 men away from the settlements. As they marched through North Carolina they heard rumors of the Cornwallis surrender at York Town. The men insisted on continuing the march. Sevier and Shelby were assigned to General Francis Marion. This was not very much to the liking of either. From Williams' **Tennessee During The Revolution**, we quote from Shelby's autobiography as used in the Greene papers and Henderson's "Isaac Shelby":

First, General Greene's letter to Shelby after Eutaw Springs Battle. It was after the September letter that Shelby and Sevier arranged to join Greene.

> *Head Quarters,*
> *High Hills of Santee*
> *Sept. 16, 1781.*

Dear Sir:

I have the pleasure to inform you that we had an action with the British Army on the 8th in which we were victorious. We took 500 prisoners in and killed and wounded a much greater number. We also took nearly 1000 stand of arms, and have driven the enemy near the gates of Charleston. I have also the pleasure to inform you that a large French fleet of nearly thirty sail of the line, has arrived in the Chesepeak bay, with a considerable number of land forces; all of which are to be employed against Lord Cornwallis, who it is suspected will endeavor to make good his retreat through North Carolina to Charleston. To prevent which I beg you to bring out as many riflemen as you can, and as soon as possible. You will march them to Charlotte, and inform me the moment you set out, and of your arrival.

If we can intercept his lordship it will put a finishing stroke to the war on the Southern states.

Should I get any intelligence which may change the face of matters I will advise you. I am with esteem and regard, your most obedient and humble servant.

Shelby gives this account of the South Carolina Campaign in his Autobiography.

I made great exertions, and collected the men in a few days thereafter, many of them had not received more than 24 hours notice and lived more than 100 miles from the place of rendezvous - but were willing to go as the call was made for a special purpose - to wit, to intercept Lord Cornwallis who it was suspected would endeavor to make good his retreat through North Carolina to Charleston and Gen. Greene thought and so did I that if we could intercept him, it would put an end to the War in the Southern states. To effect this important object, the people on the western waters were induced to volunteer their services - it was for this purpose that they were prevailed upon to leave their homes 500 miles from the scene of operations to defend a Maritime district of country surrounded with a dense population and in comparative quiet while their own fire-sides were daily menaced by the Chickamauga Indians, who as you know had declared perpetual war against the whites and could never be induced to make peace. I was far advanced on my road when I received vague information of the surrender of Cornwallis in Virginia and hesitated whether to proceed. But as the men appeared to be willing to serve out a tour of duty which at the time of entering the service I repeatedly assured them should not exceed 60 days absence from their homes, I proceeded on more leisurely to Greene, who observed to me that such a body of horse could not remain in the vicinity of his camp on account of the scarcity of forage and requested me to serve out the tour with Marion, to which I consented, however, with some reluctance as the men would be drawn 70 or 80 miles further from their homes.

Despite the news of the Cornwallis surrender, Colonels Shelby and Sevier continued their march to join Greene. The following account comes from Shelby's Autobiography.

The enemies main Southern army, it was said, lay at that time near a place called Ferguson's Swamp on the great road bearing directly to Charleston. General Marion received information several weeks after our arrival at his camp that several hundred Hessians, at a British Post near Monk's Corner, eight or ten miles below the enemies main army, were in a state of mutiny, and would surrender to any considerable American force that might appear before it; and consulted his principal officers on the propriety of surprising it, which was soon determined on and Shelby and Sevier solicited a command in it. Marion accordingly moved down eight or ten miles, and crossed over to the South side of the Santee River, from whence he made a detachment of five or six hundred men to surprise the post, the command of which was given to Colonel Mayham. The detachment consisted of Shelby's mounted riflemen with Mayham's Dragoons, about one hundred and eighty, and about twenty or thirty lowland mounted militia, the command of the whole was given to Colonel Mayham. They took up their march early in the morning, and traveled fast through the woods until late in the evening of the second day, when they struck the great road leading to Charleston, about two miles below the enemies post, which they intended to surprise. They lay upon their arms all night across the road with a design to intercept the Hessians in case the enemy had got notice of our approach and had ordered them down to Charleston before morning. In the course of the night which was dark as pitch an orderly Sergeant rode into the line amongst us, and was taken prisoner. No material papers were found upon him before he made his escape except a pocket book which contained the strength of the enemy's main army and their number then on the sick list, which was very great.

As soon as daylight appeared, we advanced to the British Post, and arrived there before sunrise. Colonel Mayham sent in one of his confidential officers with peremptory demand for a surrender of the garrison, who in a few minutes returned and reported that the officer commanding was determined to defend the post to the last extremity. Colonel Shelby then proposed that he would go in himself and make another effort to obtain a surrender, which Mayham readily consented to. Upon his approach he discovered a gap in the Abbaties, through which he rode up close to the building, when an officer opened one leaf of a long folding door. Colonel Shelby addressed him in these words: "Will you be so mad as to suffer us to storm your works; if you do, rest assured that every soul of you will be put to the sword, for there was several hundred men at hand that would soon be in with their tomahawks upon them"; he then inquired if they had any artillery. Shelby replied, "that they had guns that would blow them to pieces in a minute." Upon which the officer replied, "I suppose I must give up." Mayham seeing the door thrown wide open, and Shelby ascending the high steps to the door, immediately advanced with his dragoons and formed on the right. It was not until this moment we discovered another strong British Fort that stood five or six hundred yards to the East, and this is the first knowledge we had of that post, the garrison of which immediately marched out, about one hundred infantry and forty or fifty cavalry came around the North Angle of the fort all apparently with a design to attack us; they however soon halted as we stood firm and prepared to meet them. We took a hundred and fifty prisoners, all of them able to have fought from the window of the house, or from behind Abbaties. Ninety of them were able to stand a march to Marion's camp that day which was near sixty miles; and we paroled the remainder most of whom appeared to have been sick and unable to stand so hard a march. Information soon reached Marion's camp that the Post had been burnt down immediately on our leaving it; but it was always the opinion of Colonel Shelby that the enemy had abandoned it, and burnt it themselves, for Mayham and Shelby were the two last men that left the place, and at that time there was not the least sign of fire or smoke about it. This it is most probable they would do, as they had previously destroyed and burned down almost every building in that part of the country. This post was an immense brick building, calculated to hold a thousand men and said to have been built by Sir John Colleton a century before that period as well for defense as comfort; and was well enclosed by a strong Abbaties. In it were found, besides the prisoners, three or four hundred stand of arms, and as many new blankets. The American detachment left this post between nine and ten o'clock of the same day, and arrived at Marion's camp the night following at three o'clock. General Stewart who commanded the Enemy's main army, eight or ten miles above, made great efforts to intercept us on our return. And it was announced to Marion about sunrise next morning that the whole British army was in the old field about three miles off at the outer end of the causeway that led into his camp. Shelby was immediately ordered out with the mountain men to meet him at the edge of the swamp, to attack the enemy if he attempted to advance, and retreat at his own discretion, to where Marion would have his whole force drawn up to sustain him at an old field. Shortly after his arrival at the edge of the open plain, he observed two British officers ride up to a house equidistante between the lines; after they retired he rode to the house to know what inquiries they had made; a man told him that they had asked him when the Americans detachment had got in, what was their force, and of what troops it was composed; he replied that the detachment had come in just before day, that he had supposed as they went out they were six or eight hundred strong, and were composed chiefly of Shelby's and Sevier's mounted men, with Mayham's mounted Dragoons. The enemy, then being in the edge of the woods, slightly withdrawn out of sight, retreated back in the utmost disorder and confusion. A small party, sent out to reconnoiter the enemy, reported that many of them had thrown away their napsacks, guns and canteens. A few days afterwards General Marion received intelligence that the British commander had retreated with his whole force to Charleston. Marion's sole design in moving from the camp when the mountain men first joined them, and crossing the Santee River below; was to get within striking distance of the before mentioned post, to make (safe) the said detachment, and be able to protect and support them on their retreat if hard pushed by the enemy. After this the enemy kept so within their lines that little or no blood was spilt; and all active movements appearing to be at end, Shelby made application to General Marion for leave of absence to go the the Assembly of North Carolina, of which he was a member, and which was to meet about that time at Salem, and where he had private business of his own of the first importance. The mountain men had then but a day or two to stay, to complete their tour of duty, of sixty days, and he verily believes that they did serve it out, as he never heard to the contrary.

The Overmountain men served their sixty day enlistment. It was January, 1782 when they arrived back home. Shelby, commenting on the men, had this to say:

These mountaineers were poor men who lived by keeping stock on the range beyond the mountains; they were volunteers and neither expected or received any compensation except liquidated certificates worth two shillings in the pound. General Greene had no right nor ought to have expected to command their services. For myself, for the whole services of 1780 and 1781, both in camp and in the General Assembly, I received a liquidation certificate which my good agent in that county (Sullivan), after my removal to Kentucky, sold for six yards of middling broadcloth, and gave one coat made of it to the person who brought it out to me. Indeed I was proud of receiving that.

LAST OVERMOUNTAIN BATTLE OF REVOLUTIONARY WAR

The last Battle of the Revolutionary War, west of the Appalachian Mountains, was fought on Lookout Mountain. Bands of the Chickamauga Indians were making daily raids on frontier cabins. The Chiefs of these lower Cherokee Towns, split off from the Overhill Cherokee, had neither signed treaties nor agreed to any peace terms.

The North Carolina Legislature had authorized a campaign against this troublesome group during its 1782 July Session. Colonel Charles McDowell and Colonel John Sevier had been delegated to raise a thousand troops with which to squelch the Chickamaugas. Colonel McDowell never got around to raising a force from Burke County. Virginia, Washington County, and Sullivan County were asked to take part, but the enmity created during the Boyd's Creek Campaign, December 1780, still existed. Sevier's hurried march and battle, the Clarke-Martin fight over the cattle provided at Chote, were still resented by the Virginia and Sullivan County groups.

The final result of all this planning and conferring was a campaign led by Colonel Sevier with 250 of his Nolichucky riflemen. They left the settlements September, 1782. At Chota they were greeted by several of the leading chiefs. Two Dragging Canoe followers, John Watts and Butler, volunteered to pilot the force to the Chickamauga towns. John Watts had been stationed in the Overhill towns by Dragging Canoe, to keep him informed of the various meetings, messages and arrangements between the Overhill Chiefs and the American officials. These two guides hoped to lead Sevier and his men away from the Chickamauga Towns.

Colonel Sevier had his own ideas regarding where he planned to go. He led his force to the Middle Towns in spite of the advice of the two guides. The abandoned cabins of Bull Town, Settico, Vann's and Chickamauga were destroyed. A battle took place on Lookout Mountain. This band of Indians was outnumbered and could not match the firepower of the pioneer riflemen. The conflict was of short duration. The Chiefs of this battle are thought to have been Bloody Fellow, Wyada and Little Owl.

Colonel Sevier led his men as far south as the Coosa River. He had the vacated towns of Spring Frog, Ustinaula, Ellijay and Coosawatie destroyed. John Watts had been able to steer the troops away from the new towns of Chickamauga. Jane Iredell, a white girl held captive in the lower Towns, was brought back to her people in present Johnson County, Tennessee.

Moccasin Bend and town of Lookout Mountain as seen from the top of the mountain. Battle site of two wars.

Sevier and his men returned to Chota where a friendly conference was held with Oconostota, The Tassel, Hanging Maw and other Headmen. Thirty captives, taken during the campaign, were released to return to their homes. Majors Valentine Sevier and James Hubbard; Captains William Bean, Samuel Wear, Alexander Moore, George Russell, Neely (Cornelius) McGuire, William Smith and James Sevier were on this march, as were the Bean brothers William Jr., Robert, John, Jesse, and Edmund.

The party reached their homes in November. This expedition stopped the raids for a short while. The Chickamaugas did not molest the Washington and Sullivan County residents so much after this experience. They were learning to fear and respect the firepower of these experienced frontiersmen. This campaign did not stop the Chickamauga attacks against the Cumberland settlements.

The partisan warfare in the three most southern states continued for more than a year after Cornwallis surrendered at York Town. Most of the skirmishes were petty, but barbaric. General Washington had sent General Anthony Wayne to assist General Greene in clearing these bothersome areas. Wayne was assigned to the Georgia theatre. He drove the British-Tory groups from post to post. They were finally forced to evacuate Savannah, Georgia in July, 1782.

Charleston, South Carolina, was the last southern point to be cleared. The final skirmish took place on James Island late in 1782. It is said an American officer named Wilmont, killed there during this skirmish, was the last casualty of the Revolutionary War.

The British did not leave New York until November 25, 1783. They were placed on Staten Island and Long Island while waiting for vessels to take them away. General Henry Knox, with an American force, occupied the Bowery and Fort George on this same date. General George Washington joined them during this occupation.

A preliminary Treaty had been signed in Paris on November 30, 1782. The final Treaty was not signed until September 3, 1783. This was eight years after the first gun was fired in Lexington. Cornwallis surrendered in York Town one year and twelve days after the King's Mountain victory. It has been said that England's defeat by the Americans was her greatest victory. And for America, it can be said that her victory over England made it possible for her to conquer the whole world with her idealism of liberty for mankind. History will record how this new form of Government used its opportunity.

Council Oak, near Morganton, North Carolina, where Overmountain Men, Wilkes, Surry and Burke County Patriots discussed the Ferguson campaign that ended at King's Mountain. King's Mountain National Military Park.

Liberty Oak, at Guilford Courthouse Battle Ground. General Greene and his men camped around tree. Guilford Courthouse National Military Park.

INDEX

83

90

Roseborough, William 56
Ross, Isaac 63
Ross, John 63
Rowan County 27
Royal Empire .2
Royal Governors 5
Royal North Dragoons 54
Rudd, Burlington 63
Rumfeld, Henry 65
Russell, Andrew 56
Russell, George 56, 69, 71, 81
Russell, Moses 63
Russell, Robert 63
Russell, William 56
Rutherford, Absolom 63
Rutherford, William 63
Rutledge, John 7, 17, 18, 27
Ryerson, Samuel 54
Salem, North Carolina 47, 80
Salisbury District 67
Salisbury District Militia 27
Saluda River 50
Sample, Samuel 56, 63
Sanders 33
Sandy Plains 33
Sandy Run 30, 44
Santee 77
Santee River 50, 80
Saratoga 2, 7, 26
Sarrett, Allen 63
Savannah, Georgia 10, 82
Sawyers (Captain) 39
Sawyers, John 56, 63
Schultz, Martin 65
Scoggins, R.E. 40
Scott, Alexander 63
Scott, Arthur 63
Scott, James 63
Scott, John .63
Scott, Joseph 56, 63
Scott, Joseph Jr. 63
Scott, Robert 63
Scott, Samuel 63
Scott, Thomas 63
Scott, Walter 63
Scott, William 63
Scurlock, James 65
Second Broad River 30, 45
Self, Thomas 63
Sellers, James 63
Selman, Jeremiah 63
Settico 81
Setzer, John 65
Sevier, Abraham 63, 71
Sevier, Catherine Sherrill 20
Sevier, George Washington 54
Sevier, James 39, 52, 63, 71, 81
Sevier, John 12, 17, 19, 20, 22,
   23, 24, 25, 28, 30, 33, 34, 36, 38, 39,
   45, 46, 47, 52, 53, 54, 56, 67, 68, 69,
   70, 71, 72, 74, 75, 77, 78, 79, 80, 81
Sevier, Joseph 52, 63
Sevier, Joseph II 63
Sevier, Robert 39, 52, 56, 78
Sevier, Sarah Hawkins 12
Sevier, Valentine 13, 56, 76, 81
Shallow Ford 68
Shannon, Robert 53, 56
Shannon, Thomas 63

Sharp, Benjamin 63
Sharp, Edward 63
Sharp, James 63
Sharp, John .63
Sharp, Richard 63
Sharp, Robert 63
Sharp, Samuel 63
Sharp, Thomas E. 56, 63
Sharp, William 63
Sharpe, Ben 71
Shaver, Frederick 63
Shaver, Michael 63
Shaver, Paul 63
Shelby, David 63
Shelby, Evan 9, 78
Shelby, Evan Jr. 56
Shelby, Isaac 12, 13, 14, 15,
   16, 17, 19, 20, 24, 25, 26, 28, 29, 33,
   35, 36, 38, 39, 40, 42, 44, 45, 46, 47,
   52, 54, 56, 67, 74, 78, 79, 80, 81
Shelby, James 9, 65
Shelby, John 56, 63
Shelby, Moses 56, 63
Shelby, Thomas 63
Shell, Michael 65
Shelving Rock (Resting Place) 23
Sherrill, Adam 63, 71
Sherrill, Catherine (Bonnie Kate) . . .19
Sherrill, George 63
Sherrill, Samuel Jr. 63
Sherrill, Samuel Sr. 63
Sherrill, Uriah 65
Sherrill, William 65
Shipp, Thomas 63
Shirley, John 63
Shook, Greenbury 63
Shote, Thomas 63
Sigmon, John 56
Sigmon, Palsor 65
Silver Creek 25
Simms, James 63
Simms, John 63
Simms, Littlepage 65
Simpson, William 65
Singleton, Andrew 56
Singleton, Richard 56, 63
Siske, Bartlett 63
Siske, Daniel 63
Skaggs, Henry 63
Skaggs, John 63
Skalilosken (Prince) 50
Sloan, Alexander 63
Sloan, John .63
Sloan, William 63
Smallwood, William 63, 67
Smart, John .63
Smith's Ford 13
Smith, Daniel 56
Smith, David 63
Smith, Eaton 63
Smith, Edward 44, 63
Smith, Ezekial 65
Smith, George 63
Smith, Harnett 63
Smith, Henry 56, 63
Smith, J.M. .56
Smith, James 63
Smith, John .63
Smith, Jones 65

Smith, Leighton 63
Smith, Miner 56
Smith, Obediah 63
Smith, Phillip 63
Smith, Ransom 63
Smith, William 56, 63, 81
Smith, William B. 9
Smithers, Gabriel 65
Smoky Mountains 76
Smool, James 65
Snoddy, John 57, 63
Snodgrass, James 63
Snodgrass, William 44, 63
Somers, John 63
Sorter, William 63
South Carolina 2, 3, 6, 11,
   16, 17, 18, 27, 31, 45, 46, 47, 67, 72,
   73, 75, 77
South Mountain Gap 25
Southern Campaign 10, 43, 73
Spain 2, 3
Sparks, John 65
Speltz, John 63
Spicer, William 65
Spivey's Gap 76
Spring Frog .81
Springstone, William 69
Spruce Pine, North Carolina . . .23, 52
St. Louis 8
Stamey, John 63
Stamp Act, The 4
Stamper, Joel 65
Starnes, Nicholas 44, 63
Starnes, Peter 65
State of Franklin 20
Staten Island 82
Steed, Thomas 63
Steele, John 57, 63
Steele, Joseph 63
Steele, Samuel 63
Steele, William 63
Steen, James 57, 63
Stellars, James 63
Stencipher, Joseph 63
Step, James .30
Stephens (General) 67
Stephens, Jacob 63
Stephens, Mashack 63
Sterling, Robert 63
Steuben, Baron von 2
Stevenson, James 65
Stevenson, John 63
Stevenson, William 54
Stewart (General) 80
Stewart, James 63
Stewart, Thomas 65
Stewart, William 63
Stillwater 7
Stillwell 26
Stinson, James 57, 67, 69, 76
Stockton, George 63
Stockton, John 63
Stockton, William 63
Stone Age 51
Stone, Conway 63
Stone, Ezekial 63
Stone, Solomon 63
Stone, William 63
Stovall, Bartholomew 63